HEROES OR VILLAINS?
youth politics in the 1980s

JEREMY SEEKINGS

Research co-ordinated for JEP
by David Everatt of C A S E

Ravan Press   Johannesburg

Published by Ravan Press 1993
PO Box 31134 Braamfontein 2017
South Africa

Researched and written for
the Joint Enrichment Project
by
the Community Agency for Social Enquiry
Project co-ordinated by David Everatt

© CASE and JEP

All rights reserved. No part of this publication may be reproduced, stored in a retrieval system, or transmitted in any form or by any means, electronic, mechanical, photocopying, recording, or otherwise, without the prior permission of the copyright owners.

First published 1993

Cover design: Ingrid Obery
DTP setting and design: Ravan Press

ISBN: 0 86975 445 9

The JEP gratefully acknowledges publication support from the International Youth Foundation.

Printed by Kohler Carton & Print, Pinetown

Contents

Foreword vi
Preface viii
List of acronyms x
Introduction xi

Chapter One
   Constructing the youth 1

Chapter Two
   The youth re-emerges, 1976-84 20

Chapter Three
   Youth and township revolt, 1984-1988 .. 49

Chapter Four
   Youth in transition, 1988-92 86

Chapter Five
   Conclusion and prospects 96

Select bibliography 102
The Joint Enrichment Project 105
The Community Agency for Social Enquiry 107

Foreword

Sheila Sisulu
Director, Joint Enrichment Project

Heroes or Villains? Youth politics in the 1980s is one of a series of publications developed through research commissioned by the Joint Enrichment Project (JEP) and co-ordinated by the Community Agency for Social Enquiry (C A S E). This research is part of a process of information-gathering called for by the June 1991 inaugural conference on marginalised youth.

One of the objectives of this conference was to develop programmatic strategies to address the problems confronting young people in South Africa. In order to identify focused and effective strategies, it was necessary to define the youth, and this book is a commendable contribution to this task.

The author, Jeremy Seekings, challenges the two main stereotypes of youth: militant, disciplined and highly politicised 'young lions', or irresponsible, dangerous, reckless and ungovernable activists. He argues that youth is a political construct, which ignores many young people who are neither political nor politicised.

In developing his argument, Seekings relies almost exclusively on an examination of Congress-oriented youth groupings. For his definition of young people to be broadened, a close and in-depth examination of Black Consciousness and Pan-Africanist youth formations is an urgent priority.

Seekings' argument is fully supported by the findings of a survey undertaken by C A S E and JEP, the first ever attempt to develop a national and comprehensive portrait of young people in South Africa. This survey demonstrates that the youth are not a homogeneous, undifferentiated group. They cannot be stereotyped simply as heroes of struggle, or villains of society. They have as many different interests, needs and concerns as any other sector of society.

Millions of young South Africans are unemployed, many are under-educated, and the majority still live in conditions of abject poverty and squalor. To change this, we need to know who these young people are, and what motivates them. Seekings lays a firm basis for the development of answers to these questions.

This book is essential reading for those trying to address the problems confronting young South Africans, and those who want to understand who these young people are.

Preface

This short book is intended as a contribution to the study of youth politics and the politics of resistance in South Africa over the last two decades. It began life as a report commissioned by the Community Agency for Social Enquiry (C A S E) on behalf of the Joint Enrichment Project (JEP), a joint venture of the South African Council of Churches and Southern African Catholic Bishops Conference. A national conference on 'marginalised youth', convened by JEP in June 1991, mandated JEP to carry forward a range of activities aimed at placing youth development on the national agenda.

The initial report aimed to synthesise existing literature on youth politics in the 1980s, supplementing this with whatever other sources were available. Both the report and this book suffer from two weaknesses. Firstly, while a number of youth in leadership positions were interviewed, I have not drawn upon the oral accounts of many members of the youth at the grassroots level. The study of resistance politics in South Africa will be greatly enhanced when more of these sorts of accounts become available.

Secondly, I have focused on the mainstream of youth politics. This involves young black people (primarily African, although young coloured and Indian people are considered in passing) and specifically on the Charterist youth movement. This involves youth groups broadly oriented towards the African National Congress (ANC) and the Freedom Charter. I neglect non-Charterist youth movements – including bantustan-based groups such as the Inkatha Youth Brigade and rival opposition groups such as the Black Consciousness-oriented Azanian Students Movement (Azasm) and Azanian Youth Unity (Azanyu).

These groups have claimed huge memberships, and they need to be examined and analysed. Youth in rural areas also remains largely neglected.

This book is primarily based on the narrow range of existing research on youth politics. Huge gaps remain both in the available literature and in this book. In addition, the existing research into South African youth politics suffers from two general problems. Few academic researchers have personal experience of the subject they are examining, because most are white South Africans or not South African at all. Secondly, many aspects of youth politics have been left off the research agenda because they were regarded as too 'sensitive' in a highly polarised political context. As such, they were thought to be embarassing to the liberation movements.[1]

While writing this book, I have become increasingly aware of the many aspects of youth politics which are yet to be researched. Many of the interpretations and arguments presented here are tentatively offered, precisely because of the paucity of existing research.

I am indebted to interviewees for their time and patience, and to Monique Marks for her pertinent criticisms. I am grateful to Dr David Everatt of C A S E, who co-ordinated the entire youth project and who conceived both the report and book versions of this manuscript. Finally, my thanks to Glenn Moss and Professor Peter Randall of Ravan Press for their incisive editing.

---

1 See Seekings, J: 'South Africa's Townships, 1980-1991: An Annotated Bibliography', University of Stellenbosch, Research Unit for the Sociology of Development, Occasional Paper no. 16, February 1992.

List of acronyms

ANC	African National Congress
Ayco	Alexandra Youth Congress
Azanyu	Azanian National Youth Unity
Azasm	Azanian Students Movement
Azaso	Azanian Students Organisation
Azapo	Azanian Peoples Organisation
C A S E	Community Agency for Social Enquiry
Cayco	Cape Youth Congress
Cosas	Congress of South African Students
Cosatu	Congress of South African Trade Unions
DET	Department of Education and Training
IYCC	Inter-denoninational Youth Christian Club
IYY	International Youth Year
JEP	Joint Enrichment Project
KRO	Kagiso Residents Organisation
Malayo	Masibosane Lamontville Youth Organisation
Mayo	Mamelodi Youth Organisation
MK	Umkonto we Sizwe
Nayo	National Youth Organisation
NYO	National Youth Organisation
PAC	Pan-Africanist Congress
Peyco	Port Elizabeth Youth Congress
PWV	Pretoria-Witwatersrand-Vaal
Sasm	South African Students Movement
Saso	South African Students Organisation
Sayco	South African Youth Congress
Sayo	Saulsville-Atteridgeville Youth Organisation
Soyco	Soweto Youth Congress
TSO	Tumahole Students Organisation
UDF	United Democratic Front
YCS	Young Christian Students
YCW	Young Christian Workers

Introduction

Most accounts of South African resistance politics in the 1980s emphasise the importance of the 'youth'. Yet there is little agreement as to who or what this constitutes. This is in part due to the small number of studies focusing on 'youth politics', with youth organisation, action and attitudes remaining largely undocumented. But it is also due to underlying conceptual confusion and ambiguity.

The category of youth in South Africa is a political rather than a sociological or demographic construct. Being young is generally seen as a necessary but not a sufficient condition for inclusion in the youth; young people must also be involved in political activity to count as youth. There is also no agreement as to the age-limits of being young. It is often implied that the upper age-limit of the youth is somewhere between thirty and forty, but older people are sometimes described as youth.

Additional confusion arises from the different political criteria selected by commentators to define the kinds of activity which distinguish the youth from young people in general. As these criteria differ, so the category of youth is understood in different ways. Furthermore, as the political context changes, so the salience of different criteria change. Thus, the category of youth has meant different things to different people, and different things at different times.

Amidst almost infinite diversity, however, two stereotypical views of the youth recur. These I refer to as the apocalyptic and liberatory stereotypes. The apocalyptic view of the youth is essentially hostile, identifying the youth with violence and destruction. The liberatory view of the youth, in contrast, is broadly sympathetic, seeing the youth as the 'comrades' or 'young lions' who selflessly struggled for liberation and democracy. Over the last twenty-odd years one or both of these views have underpinned the predominant perception of youth in journalistic and academic accounts of the youth in South Africa.

While the criteria used to define the youth are varied and changing, they revolve around the political factors of either association with violent direct action or commitment to fundamental political change. The category of youth is almost exclusively used to refer to young African people. It sometimes includes young coloured and Indian people, but rarely young white South Africans. As Everatt observes, South Africa has white teenagers, but black youth.[1] Teenager is a term devoid of political meaning; youth is laden with it.

This book examines the construction and reconstruction of this category of youth in South Africa since the mid-1970s, and surveys the changing forms of political organisation and action which have characterised this fluid group of people. It considers only those young people involved in radical political organisation and protest, or in political violence (even when participants have not identified themselves as youth).

The predominant understanding of the category of youth has changed over time, with the liberatory view of the youth initially gaining influence but later being engulfed by a resurgent apocalyptic view. Between the mid-1970s and the present, we have turned almost full circle: in both periods the youth have been viewed widely with more concern than favour, while in the intervening period of the mid-1980s the youth were often portrayed in glowing terms.

During the 1970s the category of youth was rarely used in political discourses. Politically active young black South Africans were often involved in student organisations, and most of the protesters of 1976-77 were identified as students or even school children. The term youth was generally reserved for unidentified young people who engaged in morally questionable forms of direct action. Even after the 1976-77 uprisings (the so-called Soweto

---

[1] See David Everatt's 'Introduction' to the C A S E national survey of youth in South Africa, undertaken for the JEP (forthcoming).

Introduction

Revolt, although many other townships were involved), ex-students chose to describe themselves as students participating in ostensibly student organisation, rather than as members of the youth.

Chapter One of this book examines and tries to clarify the concept of the youth with respect to South Africa since the mid-1970s. The two predominant stereotypes of the youth in the context of resistance politics in South African are examined. Neither stereotype has any sociological or demographic basis, while both refer to sociologically disparate individuals who have particular forms of political behaviour in common.

Chapter One also outlines the social and economic experiences of young people in general. The patterns of youth politics cannot, however, be reduced to these experiences alone. Youth politics also needs to be understood in terms of the political context, which largely shapes the ways in which the category of youth is itself constructed out of the broader grouping of young people. Subsequent chapters illustrate this for successive periods.

The category of youth was reconstructed in the aftermath of, and largely because of, the 1976-77 uprisings. Chapter Two examines this reconstruction of the youth in the period between 1976 and 1984. The key changes occurred in 1980-82 when the term youth was imbued with new liberatory content. Several problems emerged for the former students of 1976-77 who continued to organise themselves through student structures, and separate youth organisations were formed to accommodate them. In the early 1980s the term 'youth' was largely used to refer to the small number of better-schooled students who had been radicalised during 1976-77 and remained politically active thereafter.

This process of reconstruction of the category of youth was part-and-parcel of broader processes of transition in opposition politics, with the revival and rapid growth of a militant and ANC-aligned network of activists and organisations inside the country. During this period the youth were not the major force in political action, nor were they seen as such. But the newly-formed youth congresses and other organisations played a growing role in this nascent ANC-aligned movement.

The youth became a key political force during the township and rural revolt of 1984-1987. Chapter Three examines the further reconstruction of the category of youth during this period of revolt. Sympathetic observers viewed direct action as indicative of political commitment to the cause of national liberation. The category of youth was thus expanded through the inclusion of very large numbers of young black South Africans. But the character, goals and motivations of this youth were rather more complex than the crude liberatory stereotype implied. Chapter Three examines the diversity embraced within the category of youth in this period.

Chapter Three also traces the development of formal youth organisation at national level, culminating in the formation of the South African Youth Congress (Sayco) in 1987, and at the local level, where youth congresses and other organisations proliferated. During the township revolt the character of formal youth organisations at the local level changed, reflecting the shifting prominence of different groups of youth.

There has been another partial reconstruction of the category of youth in the aftermath of the township revolt. The changing political context involved a steady demobilisation of the youth in political terms (with short-lived upturns in 1989 and early 1990). At the same time, there has been an upsurge in violent action. The liberatory view of the youth has thus lost ground, with the apocalyptic view again becoming more prominent. Chapter Four explores these issues, as well as the later aspects of youth in transition, in particular the transformation of Sayco and its component youth congress into the relaunched ANC Youth League and its local branches.

Throughout this study, the phrase 'youth politics' is used with caution. As the category of youth is politically constructed, it is somewhat absurd to refer to 'youth politics' as if the organisations, activities and attitudes involved can be separated from the assumptions which underlie their selection in the first place. There is no such thing as 'youth politics' in terms of a discrete, let alone homogeneous, sociological category of people which thinks, organises and acts, politically, in specific and distinctive ways. 'Youth politics' contrasts with, for example, 'working class politics' because the latter refers to the political behaviour of a discrete (albeit hardly homogeneous) category. The youth do not form a

Introduction

conceptually comparable collective group.

'Youth politics' is therefore used in a general descriptive sense only. The analysis of youth politics must examine the basis of the construction of the category of youth. It must identify who actually comprises the youth as well as exploring the details of youth organisation and action. Use of the term 'youth' can all too easily obscure as much as it reveals about resistance politics and contemporary social issues.

Chapter One

Constructing the youth

The ambiguity attached to the category of youth is probably greater in South Africa than elsewhere, but it is rooted in an ambiguity fundamental to the very concept of youth. Youth has a dual meaning in everyday usage in the English language, referring to either age or the attributes generally associated with age.

Youth refers to the period in people's lives between childhood and adulthood. One aspect of this is age: the youth comprise certain age cohorts, that is *young* people. But childhood and adulthood cannot be reduced to age. The boundary between youth and adulthood is generally understood in terms of rituals of initiation or other rites of passage to adulthood such as marriage, parenthood or possibly employment. These experiences are assumed to transform peoples' attitudes and behaviour. When youth go through this transition they are thought to become more responsible, cautious, even conservative. Youth thus refers to particular attitudes and behaviour, including such supposed characteristics as enthusiasm and inexperience. As such, older people are sometimes referred to as being youthful.

South Africa underwent considerable social change in the 1980s; childhood, youth and adulthood became blurred as the 'natural' progression from home to school, and then to work became anything but commonplace. In this context the category of youth came to be increasingly understood in terms of attitudes and behaviour, particularly related to the process of political change. This has given rise to stereotyped understandings of the youth, with each stereotype based in an interpretation of the broader processes of political change.

Two stereotypes of the youth were widespread during the 1980s. One was essentially sympathetic, the other hostile. The first portrayed the youth as politicised and militant, the second as destructive and rebellious.[1] Both stereotypes characterised the youth in terms of certain forms of behaviour and the motivations and effects which are associated with these. The composition of the youth remained unclear. Both these 'apocalyptic' and 'liberatory' stereotypes shared an underlying view of the youth as militant, impatient and lacking caution.

These stereotypes are, of course, over-simplifications. They do not necessarily correspond to the self-perceptions of members of the youth. But examining them better reveals the political criteria which recur in the construction of the category of youth.

This study is concerned with those organisations and actions generally characterised as involving youth. The problematic term 'youth' is thus used here according to conventional psychological-cum-behavioral characterisations. But the term 'youth' is not synonymous with 'young people'. This chapter does not assume that all young people share the psychological or behavioral characteristics of the 'youth'. The term 'youth' is used descriptively rather than analytically: the composition or identity, motivation and organisation of different 'youth' needs to be empirically established. In short, 'youth' is the starting point for analysis rather than analysis in itself.

Youth as apocalypse

One widespread stereotype of the youth portrays them as rebels against political and social order, and associated with violence and

---

[1] See also Sitas, A: 'The Making of the Comrades Movement in Natal 1985-91', *Journal of Southern African Studies* 18/3 (September 1992), p. 3.

destruction. In the 1980s their militancy was primarily directed into the struggle against the apartheid state, although even then township residents were among the victims. Now, it is feared, that militancy and violence is flowing into crime and gangsterism, in a struggle no longer against the 'system' but against 'society' itself. Ari Sitas has written about this stereotype with respect to the 'comrades':

> The tyre, the petrol-bomb, the knife, the stone, the hacking: death. The words 'comrade' and 'amaqabane' conjure them up ... The word [comrade] frames images of unemployed black youth with no future, no home, busy destroying everything in their way: homes, shops, schools, infrastructures and traditions ... [T]he media picture is of young men, hungry men, with hardened features and red eyes ... [2]

In this view the youth are not only associated with violent behaviour; violence is largely understood in terms of the youth. Reasonable, responsible people – adults, perhaps – are not violent; violent and disorderly behaviour can only be attributed to deviance or irresponsibility, exemplified by the youth. This view is not only widespread, but persistent, running through the history of urban struggles in South Africa. Consider the following account of urban rioting:

> It was particularly apt that the urge to destruction and brutality should have been expressed primarily through the medium of tsotsi youths. Offspring of temporary and shiftless liaisons ... they had come into the world unwelcomed and unloved ... born into disease, squalor and inadequate homes ... Among these young people were the halt and the maimed, the dagga-smokers and shebeen-frequenters, a few sub-mental cases, several with previous convictions; as well as some of good character who were swept in on impulse. Rejected alike by the society which spawned them and by the economy in which they had no place, these children distilled in their moment of frenzy all the bitterness felt by their community at large against those who appeared to crush and exploit them ... The tsotsis, unlike the

---

2   Sitas, A: 'The Comrades', *Reality* (May 1991), p. 6.

majority of adults present at the time, were able to strike in an ecstasy of abandon, with no property, no future, no employment, nothing to lose save their seemingly worthless lives.[3]

This account dates not from the 1980s, but from 1961, and refers to the 1952 riots in East London.

The perception of menacing black youth clearly predates the 1980s. It seems to be the product of rapid twentieth century urbanisation and industrialisation, and has changed as the black urban population itself has grown. La Hausse, for example, describes the *amalaita* gangs of young migrant workers in Durban in the early decades of the century.[4] These were succeeded in the apocalyptic imagination by the *tsotsi* gangs of the 1940s and 1950s.[5] From the mid-1970s it was simply the youth who posed the threat. Now, in the 1990s, the spectre of an apocalyptic 'lost generation' of 'marginalised youth' looms menacingly over any political and constitutional settlement, threatening to devour a post-apartheid democracy.

This view of the youth combines the racist imageries of African 'idleness'[6] and savagery (feared by white South Africans for so long), with the western tradition of urban male criminality and the associated fear of generational rebellion. Violence, together with rape and dispossession, is threatened by a group defined as deviant, uneducated, irresponsible and uncontrolled.

As Straker has pointed out, treating the youth as psychopathological turns them from victims into villains.[7] In more

---

3   Reader, DH: *The Black Man's Portion: history, demography and living conditions in the native locations of East London, Cape Province* (Cape Town: Oxford University Press, 1961) p. 28. 'Halt' means defective or lame.

4   La Hausse, P: '"Mayihlome": Towards an understanding of Amalaita gangs in Durban, c1900-1930', in Clingman, S (ed): *Regions and Repertoires: topics in South African politics and culture* (Johannesburg: Ravan, 1991).

5   See especially Glaser, C: 'Anti-Social Bandits: juvenile delinquency and the tsotsi youth gang sub-culture on the Witwatersrand, 1935-1960', MA dissertation, University of the Witwatersrand (1990).

6   See Coetzee, JM: 'Idleness in South Africa', *Social Dynamics*, 8/1 (1982).

7   Straker, G: 'From victim to villain: a sleight of speech? Media

general terms, labeling protesters as 'youth' serves to delegitimate them and their actions. The label implies irresponsibility, even irrationality, and disregards the issues which sparked the protest. It projects a stigmatising identity, criminalises protest and legitimates repression.

The label 'youth' suggests more than just 'young'. The perception that young people are less responsible for their actions pervades the judicial system, for example, where age has generally been regarded as a mitigating factor in sentencing. 'Youth' has inherent connotations of destructiveness, immaturity, impulsiveness and even susceptibility. Conservative commentaries on conflict in South Africa equate youth with violence, and emphasise the susceptibility of the youth to political manipulation.[8]

Apocalyptic portrayals of South Africa's township youth sometimes compared them with the Khmer Rouge of Cambodia, even referring to them as the 'Khmer Noir':

> *They kill. They rape ... like the Khmer Rouge of Cambodia, they are greatly feared and their intimidation largely works. And, like the Khmer Rouge, it's all done in the names of 'justice' and 'liberation'.*[9]

In the more extreme versions of this view, the youth had become synonymous with savagery. There is, of course, evidence linking contemporary township violence with young people. And the concern with the youth is not confined to white South Africans – many black journalists, political leaders and ordinary township residents have warned of the problems posed by disorderly youth. But reducing the youth to participation in violence ignores other forms of political action.

---

representations of townships youth', *South African Journal of Psychology*, 19/1 (1989).

8 See Campbell, K: *Children of the Storm: The Abuse of Children for the Promotion of Revolution* (Halfway House: Lonetree Publications, 1987); Roux, H: *How Revolutionaries Use Children* (Halfway House: Lonetree Publications, 1988).

9 Bridgland, F: 'Young comrades are rocking the boat with power play', *Daily Despatch,* 6 November 1990.

The youth as 'young lions'

The liberatory view of the youth, in contrast with the apocalyptic view, focuses on the political commitment of the youth and their contribution in the struggle for justice and liberation. While the apocalyptic view of the youth portrays them as disorderly, destructive and self-serving, the liberatory view depicts them as purposeful and altruistic. Rather than being anti-social predators, they are political rebels spearheading the people's struggle. They are highly politicised, rather than inadequately socialised. They are for and within, rather than against, the 'community'.

In this stereotype, the youth were lauded as 'young lions', and urged to 'roar'. In 1987, for example, the ANC called on the youth to 'act as the yeast, to energise and dynamise the people as a whole'. Two years later, Sayco stated: 'It is ... the youth who form the core of the "political" and "military" armies of the revolution'.[10] The role of the youth within township politics was seen as similar to that of Umkhonto we Sizwe within the ANC.

Just as the apocalyptic youth of the mid-1980s had a long historical pedigree, so the liberatory youth stood in a tradition of militant and radical 'youth' in liberation politics, stretching back to the ANC Youth League of the 1940s and early 1950s. And just as there had been changes in the character of the apocalyptic youth, so there had been important shifts in the perceived composition of the liberatory youth. Proponents of the liberatory view had to characterise the youth precisely because political organisations, including the ANC and its internal allies, were concerned to organise them. The youth needed to be identified and their role in the struggle 'correctly' theorised if the appropriate organisation was to be developed.

In the 1940s the Youth League primarily comprised educated activists, and did not organise a mass base.[11] In the mid-1970s the

---

10 *Sechaba* (February 1987), p. 10; Sayco: 'Memorandum on the building of the ANC Youth League', May 1990, p. 3.
11 Glaser, C: 'Students, tsotsis and the Congress Youth League: youth organisation on the Rand in the 1940s', *Perspectives in Education* 10/2 (1988/89).

'youth' were contrasted with 'students' – and the protests of 1976 were generally attributed to 'our children' or 'school children'.[12] The youth were seen as comprising ex-students who remained active after leaving university or school (although many such youth inside the country saw themselves as students, albeit not school-going students, and were organised in student structures, as we shall see below).

By 1981 students were being included in the category of 'youth'. The ANC declared 1981 as 'Year of the Youth', and referred to 'the millions of our youth inside the country – students, working people, the youth in the rural areas, young women, young Christians' (interestingly, unemployed youth were not mentioned). This diversity had to be explained in terms of the ANC's class analysis of South African society. 'The youth are not and should not be viewed as a class', the ANC advised, 'but as a social group (which is not homogeneous) that corresponds fully to the social structure of a given society'.[13] For both strategic and theoretical reasons the ANC was opposed to the view that students or the youth could be the backbone of the liberation struggle. The ANC therefore emphasised the 'working youth' within the wider category of youth.

This official ANC view of the youth was reproduced, with additions, in documents prepared and discussed for or by ANC-oriented youth organisations inside the country. For example, according to a document discussed at a 1986 workshop preparing for the formation of Sayco:

> [T]he youth as a group does not form a class but they are a social strata [sic] (sector). And, unlike other economic strata such as the petty bourgeoisie, the youth are not undifferentiated and homogeneous.[14]

---

12 See *Sechaba* (August 1979), for example.
13 *Sechaba* (March 1981); 'Youth and the Freedom Charter' in *Sechaba*, (April 1981), p. 11.
14 'The Theory of the South African Revolution', paper prepared for Sayco preparatory workshop, 25/26 October 1986. See also Stofile, N: 'The Role of the Youth in the Liberation Struggle' (*State vs Baleka and others*, court exhibit C6, and anon: 'The Youth in the Democratic Movement', court exhibit C7.

Later documents identified the following 'gradations amongst the youth': 'The working youth; the student youth; the rural and peasant youth; the unemployed youth; intellectuals; exploiters.' The youth thus included both 'the haves and the have-nots'; their loyalties, aspirations and struggles varied, mirroring the class, religious and other divisions that characterise society as a whole.[15] Unemployed youths, intellectuals and exploiters were added to the 1981 breakdown of the youth (possibly because ANC-aligned youth organisations had developed stronger roots among white youth and especially unemployed township youth during the 1980s). But what was to unite these varied – and changing – elements of the youth? Certain characteristics common to the youth were identified in a 1990 document:

☆ the youth represent the future for all classes and social strata;
☆ youth is a 'crucial and pivotal' stage in people's lives of 'avidly searching for a rational understanding of the surrounding world'; 'the youth therefore displays curiosity, rebelliousness, impassioned and uncontrollable enthusiasm; it quickly forms judgements and abandons others';
☆ the youth are 'determined, impatient and displays zeal and nerve in fighting for what [they] conceive as just.' Within each class, the youth are therefore the 'shock troops', the 'driving force' and 'dynamo';
☆ however, 'due to their inexperience and illusions bred of their psychological make-up, young people can be easily swayed into positions that are counter to their interests.' It is even the case that, 'not seldom, young people are enticed *en masse* to adopt social and cultural values alien and often detrimental to their interests.'[16]

Peter Mokaba, president of Sayco (1987-91) and then of the ANC Youth League (since 1991), argued in an interview that

> *A youth can be a person who is married, who is working, a person who is still a student ... There are women, there are workers, there are intellectuals ... But there are characteristics*

---

15 Sayco: 'Memorandum', p. 1.
16 Sayco: 'Memorandum', p. 2.

which would always distinguish them from all other sectors of the community ... The militancy is part of it ... The way in which they regard the world, their ability to take on new ideas and develop the older ones that they believed in ... One of the characteristics also is mobility ... They are critical, they have a critical approach to life. They are not afraid to confront new situations.[17]

The liberatory view understood the youth in widely-encompassing terms; in organisational practice, however, the youth were more precisely conceptualised. Militancy and politicisation were understood in terms of taking on the system outside of the workplace or the school. Militant workers actively struggling over working conditions and wages through trade unions, and militant students campaigning over educational grievances within the school, were rarely regarded as youth in organisational terms. The membership of youth congresses included students and workers, but their concerns as youth lay outside the school and workplace. Industrial, educational and civic struggles may have been fundamentally political, but for the youth, more overtly or explicitly political struggles should take precedence whenever conditions made this possible.

As resistance and conflict broadened during the 1980s, so the understanding of what constituted political resistance, and of who comprised the youth, broadened. The physical militancy of many younger people in township streets was interpreted as indicating an underlying politicisation, however crude. The streetfighter joined the articulate activist among the youth. Officially the workers were still identified as the pillar of the struggle, but it was the youth on the township streets who were actually liberating the country. As we shall see in Chapter Three, the numbers of people who were in the youth grew rapidly, and their composition changed.

The liberatory understanding of the youth is reflected in sympathetic academic writing. In an early study, tellingly entitled 'The Soldiers of Luthuli', Johnson writes that 'youth refers to an attitude of mind as much as it does to age. It connotes the most energetic, volatile and impatient elements of the black communi-

---

17   Interview, April 1992.

ties'.[18] Zulu similarly suggests that politics is central to the self-definition of the 'youth'.[19]

Research amidst the stereotypes

The apocalyptic and liberatory stereotypes of the youth overlap as well as differ. Both see the youth as curious and rebellious, militant and impatient, impulsive and impressionable. It is in ascribing motivations and interpreting the accompanying behaviour that the stereotypes differ. Sympathetic commentators emphasised that the youth were highly politicised, and that their actions were therefore purposive and ordered as an explicit and considered part of the liberation struggle. Unsympathetic (and often fearful) commentators, on the other hand, emphasised violent action. This was seen as inherently irresponsible, and therefore lacking either purpose or order. Both approaches were often interpreting the actions of, and ascribing contrasting motivations to, the same people. Both stereotypes characterised youth in behavioral and psychological, rather than sociological or demographic terms.

Several scholars have uneasily focused on this overlap between the two views of the youth. They have moved beyond blanket condemnation or celebration, and identified both negative and positive features of the youth. Bundy discusses the 'immediatism' of the urban youth in the mid-1980s, describing it as 'an impatient anticipation of imminent victory, a hubristic assessment of progress made, and a naive underestimation of the resources of the state.' He suggests that there is

> *an essential dualism to youth politics: on the one hand, it is characteristically militant and dynamic; on the other hand, by its nature it is short on theoretical sophistication and*

---

18 Johnson, S: 'The Soldiers of Luthuli: Youth in the Politics of Resistance in South Africa', in Johnson, S (ed): *South Africa: no turning back* (London: Macmillan, 1988), p. 95.
19 Zulu, P: 'The youth in extra-parliamentary opposition', in Giliomee, H and Schlemmer, L (eds): *Negotiating South Africa's Future* (Halfway House: Southern Books, 1989), p. 95.

experience. Youth/student politics in a time of crisis is a hybrid of precocity and immaturity.[20]

Hyslop writes that the 'triumphalism' of the youth often inhibited organisation and alliance-building. Their 'adventurism' shook the state, but also led to disunity and terror within townships; the movement of resistance threatened to 'devour' itself.[21] But these studies also fail to examine carefully who they are writing about.

There is little readily available evidence on how the category of youth is generally understood in South Africa's townships and rural areas. Some indication is provided in a series of interviews conducted in 1990-91 in Tumahole, a township outside Parys in the northern Orange Free State. The responses suggest that the youth were understood primarily in terms of public, although not necessarily political, activity. Each of the fifty-eight interviewees, who ranged in age from sixteen to seventy years, was asked who was a youth. The most important criterion which emerged in the answers given involved the level of public activity, whether in sports, church, politics or other areas. Many of the interviewees suggested that an active person remained a youth even when aged fifty, sixty or even seventy. Youths are 'very active, in a hurry for life, [who] like the fast lane' said one. 'Somebody who is not a youth is the one who is lazy, unable to think, always tired', said another. Nelson Mandela was cited as an example of an elderly youth![22]

---

20 Bundy, C: 'Street sociology and pavement politics: some aspects of student/youth consciousness during the 1985 schools crisis in Greater Cape Town', *Journal of Southern African Studies* 13/3 (April 1987), pp. 322-3, 330.
21 Hyslop, J: 'Student school movements and state education policy, 1972-87', in Cobbett, W and Cohen, R (eds): *Popular Struggles in South Africa Today* (London: James Currey, 1988), pp. 193-8.
22 Seekings, J: 'Report on Preliminary Study of Female Youth in Tumahole, O.F.S.' (University of Stellenbosch, February 1991) and 'Second Report on Preliminary Study of Female Youth in Tumahole, O.F.S.' (University of Stellenbosch, January 1992). See also Straker, G: *Faces in the Revolution: the psychological effects of violence on township youth in South Africa* (Cape Town: David Philip, 1992), p. 19.

There is a clear need for research into the self-perceptions of youth, and into the views of the youth held by other people on the ground. When such research is completed it might be possible to reconstruct the category of youth in ways which better combine observers' and participants' views. In the meanwhile, existing stereotypes of the youth cannot be avoided.

Socio-economic factors

Youth politics in the period under discussion was framed by the social and economic experiences of young people in general. These experiences have been widely documented elsewhere and are only outlined here.

About two out of three young African people lived in rural areas (regardless of whether 'young' is defined as ten to thirty-four years old, or fifteen to twenty-four). Most lived in the Transvaal (together with its bantustans). About one-quarter lived in Natal/KwaZulu. Of the metropolitan areas, only the PWV contained a significant proportion of young African people within the total population. As such, we should avoid regarding the urban 'youth' as typical of young black South Africans.[23]

A growing number of young black South Africans was absorbed into the education system in the late 1970s and early 1980s. The body of African secondary school students more than tripled between 1975 and 1984, with the number of matriculants growing almost tenfold. This rapid expansion had three important social consequences:

☆ the failure to improve the quality of schooling generated discontent within the schools;
☆ the sluggish performance of the economy meant that many students were unable to find a job they considered appropriate when they left school; and

---

23   1980 Population Census, Central Statistical Office. The definition of rural in the census includes peri-urban areas, incorporating many squatter settlements.

☆ the expansion of schooling involved an expansion of the most overtly politicised section of the population.[24]

Despite the growing numbers of students, many young people were not attending school. In 1980, a maximum of eighty-two per cent of ten to fourteen year-olds were registered students. Of the fifteen to nineteen year-olds, only forty per cent were registered students, and of the twenty to twenty-four year-olds, just five per cent were students. An estimated two million young people between the ages of seven and sixteen were not attending school in 1988. One-third of a million children were dropping out of school each year before completing Standard Four, and almost a quarter of a million people dropped out of secondary school each year. Failure rates were very high at all levels. The political conflict of the mid-1980s further disrupted schooling. Besides boycotts, the quality of teaching fell within schools, and in some areas schools were burnt down.[25]

Leaving school was rarely followed by employment. The economic slow-down and recession of the early 1980s resulted in escalating unemployment. Schlemmer reports that he was not aware of any survey which showed over fifteen per cent of sixteen to twenty-four year-olds in formal employment.[26] Unemployment occurred across the African population, but high school leavers fared particularly badly:

---

24 See Bundy: 'Street sociology' and Hyslop: 'School student movements'.
25 These percentages are calculated from the 1980 Annual Report of the Department of Education and Training and the 1980 Population Census – they should be regarded as overestimates; Hartshorne, K: 'Education and employment', in Everatt, D and Sisulu, E (eds): *Black Youth in Crisis: facing the future*, (Johannesburg: Ravan, 1992); in East London's Duncan Village, ten out of eleven schools were burnt down in August 1985 during a period of intense conflict. See Kruger, F: 'DET destroys education in Duncan Village', *Work in Progress* 45 (November/December 1986); also Gultig, J and Hart, M: '"The world is full of blood": Youth, schooling and conflict in Pietermaritzburg, 1987-1989', *Perspectives in Education* 11/2 (1990).
26 Schlemmer, L: mimeo, August 1991, p. 3.

> *They have been thrust onto the labour market at precisely the moment that it has been contracting: many are too highly educated for cheap or unskilled labour; and white collar openings are increasingly the preserve of those who manage to attain tertiary education.*[27]

A national survey found that unemployment was the second most widely cited problem among young people (behind teenage pregnancies). School-leavers generally waited for three years before finding their first job. Many young people shifted from job to job, retrenchment to retrenchment, in both the formal and informal sectors. Hartshorne emphasises that in the early 1990s many young people are not only unemployed, but are probably unemployable, given their lack of skills and educational qualifications, and the poor prospects of the economy for the foreseeable future.[28]

The position of young people within both the household and the 'community' seems to have shifted in response to these broader social processes, together with politicisation and rising violence. The proliferation of gangs in coloured areas in the Western Cape in the 1970s has been attributed to the destruction of old coloured 'communities' through removals under the Group Areas Act.[29]

Ramphele writes of 'the rapid downward spiral towards total disintegration of the fabric of the black community', while Mokwena refers to a 'crisis of authority in black communities'. The declining authority of older men in both household and 'community' was associated with a resurgence of assertive youth cultures.

---

27 Bundy: 'Street sociology', p. 312.
28 Moller, V: 'Lost Generation Found: Black Youth at Leisure', *Indicator SA*, Issue Focus (May 1991), pp. 11, 28; Hartshorne: 'Education and employment'.
29 Pinnock, D: *The Brotherhoods: Street Gangs and State Control in Cape Town* (Cape Town: David Philip, 1984). See also Scharf, W: 'The Impact of Liquor on the Working-Class (with Particular Focus on the Western Cape)', MSocSci dissertation, University of Cape Town (1984/85); also Scharf, 'The resurgence of urban street gangs and community responses in Cape Town during the late eighties', in Hansson, D and Van Zyl Smit, D (eds): *Towards Justice? Crime and state control in South Africa* (Cape Town: Oxford University Press, 1990).

Mokwena writes of the emergence in the late 1980s of a 'survivalistic' youth culture, in which violence was endorsed as a means of procuring scarce material resources.[30]

Structural context and political behaviour

Most accounts of 'youth politics' adopt an essentially structural account of a (largely undifferentiated) 'youth', focusing on high levels of unemployment and the inadequacies of schooling. As Bundy writes, in an oft-quoted passage:

> *Take politically rightless, socially subordinate, economically vulnerable youths; educate them in manners beyond their parents' wildest dreams, put them in educationally grotesque institutions; ensure that their awareness is shaped by punitive social practices in the world beyond the schoolyard – and then dump them in large numbers on the economic scrap-heap.*[31]

Such accounts attach little importance to organisational factors or to the immediate political dynamics of the situation. This has been variously criticised. For example, Diseko comments:

> *Although socio-economic, political and educational factors are important to grasp, focusing primarily on them tends to rob black resistance of its own momentum and its ability to initiate and create space for itself even under the most hostile conditions.*[32]

---

30 Ramphele, M: 'Social disintegration in the black community: implications for social transformation', and Mokwena, S: 'Living on the wrong side of the law: marginalisation, youth and violence', both in Everatt and Sisulu: *Black Youth in Crisis*.
31 Bundy: 'Street sociology', p. 313.
32 Diseko, N: 'Student Organisation and the Education Struggle in South Africa, 1979-85', paper presented at a conference on Economic Change, Social Conflict and Education in Contemporary South Africa, Grantham, UK, March 1989. See also Matona, T: 'Student Organisation and Political Resistance in South Africa: an analysis of the Congress of South African Students, 1979-1985', honours dissertation, University of Cape Town (1992).

The role of organisation, both formal and informal, needs to be examined. More broadly, the relationship between youth, their behaviour, and macro-phenomena such as high unemployment, needs carefully scrutiny. The youth (among others) need to be treated as actors in a meaningful sense, and not simply the bearers of structural conditions such as education, employment or political crises. Neither political behaviour nor violence can be explained solely in terms of underlying structural conditions; behaviour is too contingent on immediate experiences and context. These may themselves be shaped by general conditions, but are not determined by them. General structural accounts explain everything and, therefore, nothing.

It remains unclear whether social or economic hardship particularly affected those young people whose behaviour led to them being considered as youth. Many studies describe the youth as motivated by these structural factors. This view rests on the assumption that most young people were youth. Straker unusually makes this assumption quite explicit:

> *Certainly among the youth it was the majority who participated in the eruptions. The youngster who did not participate in these popular uprisings was the exception rather than the rule.*[33]

Unfortunately, Straker does not clarify what she means by 'participation' in the uprisings. Does she include marching in demonstrations? Involuntarily boycotting school? Observing a consumer boycott by not shopping at the targeted shops?

Few studies clearly identify who falls within the category of youth. Young people are frequently regarded as one monolithic group. Bundy writes about 'youth politics', but his discussion of young people in Cape Town is limited to school students.[34] Other writers imply that they are talking about a smaller group.

Hartshorne, for example, writes:

> *[T]he great majority are unemployed, most are 'politicised' (but not necessarily with the same 'politics'); most have grown up in*

---

33 Straker: *Faces in the Revolution*, p. 19.
34 Bundy: 'Street sociology'; see similarly Hyslop: 'School student movements'.

a culture of violence and are no strangers to it; and most, in educational terms, have a sense of failure.[35]

Several other South African studies, however, point to the diversity of young people. Moller notes that 'the most powerful images projected by the media are South African youth outside work and school.' She continues:

> *Media images and the literature on youth culture tend to show youth at their most active and most destructive ... There is a need to balance the picture by exposing the full range of activities in which youth participate, actions as well as idleness and daydreaming, creativity as well as destruction.*

Moller proceeds to illustrate this diversity of activity. She reports that young people had mixed feelings about political activity. Most saw this as essential, but were wary of many forms of involvement. In contrast with Straker, Moller writes:

> *Attending rallies, possibly the most publicised youth activity of the 1980s, is a specialist activity. Only one quarter of the surveyed youth stated they went to rallies on a monthly basis. The remainder attended youth rallies less often than one per annum if at all.*[36]

Let us consider some of the numbers involved. The South African Youth Congress variously claimed about half-a-million members, and up to two million supporters – but even the latter figure represents less than one in four African people nationwide aged between fifteen and thirty-four (and Sayco's affiliates included some people less than fifteen, as well as coloured, Indian and even some white members). Moller points to the differences between young men and women, between working and unemployed young people, between church-going and politicised young people, and

---

35 Hartshome: 'Education and employment'.
36 Moller: 'Lost Generation Found', p. 24. See also Inkatha Institute: 'The Circumstances of the Black Urban Youth in South Africa' (May 1990); and Woods, G: 'Rebels with a cause: the discontent of black youth', *Indicator SA* 7/1 (Summer 1989).

between young people from different types of settlement.[37]

Attitude surveys indicate that the 'typical' young person is very different to either of the two common stereotypes of the youth. Schlemmer reports on research which suggested that

> *typical young people in the townships are not over-politicised or hyper-radicalised, deviant, amoral or anti-social. They have huge problems; huge disadvantages ... but they are certainly not as alienated in terms of their own commitments as most stereotypes would suggest.*

Young people's views on politics, violence and so on, were little different to those of older people. Schlemmer continues:

> *There is undoubtedly a minority among youth which is anti-social, deeply enmeshed in gang culture and which has a criminal predisposition. There is also a minority of youth which may be characterised by 'organised or semi-organised' socio-political alienation ... [who] may be at least available for confrontation and violence in the township ... these are minorities. One dare not understand all township youth in these terms. The passive majority remains largely invisible.*[38]

Another survey makes similar points, identifying discrete groups of young black South Africans, including 'socialites', 'strivers', 'traditionalists' and so on.[39]

These findings should not be surprising. International studies generally indicate that a plurality of youth cultures exist, with rebellious youth defining themselves not only in relation to the authority against which they rebel, but also against other young people whom they see as conformist. In other words, rebellious youth cultures are (at least partially) defined in relation to more conservative youth cultures. Willis, in his renowned study of working class boys in the English Midlands, found that the rebellious 'lads' contrasted themselves with the conformist 'ear-oles'

---

37 Moller: 'Lost Generation Found'.
38 Schlemmer: mimeo, p. 3
39 The survey (by Markinor) was reported in the *Sunday Times*, 21 June 1992.

(so named because they actually listened to teachers in the classroom!). Similar findings are reported in other international studies.[40]

Various studies suggest that neither 'political' youth nor 'anarchic' youth constitute a majority of the total population of young people. In the South African context the youth comprise a particular section, perhaps even a large one, of young people. They are characterised by behaviour or motivation and not according to demographic status.

The following chapters examine the forms of organisation and action which characterise this particular group of young people.

---

40 Willis, P: *Learning to Labour: how working-class kids get working-class jobs* (Farnborough: Saxon House, 1977). Monique Marks has pointed out a significant difference between the situation studied by Willis and that in South Africa: Willis' rebels rejected schooling, in contrast to many of South Africa's protesting students who have demanded better education.

Chapter Two

The youth re-emerge, 1976-84

The youth re-emerged as a central category in political opposition in the 1980s. The ANC Youth League had played an important role between the mid-1940s and mid-1950s, but the category of youth remained largely peripheral to political organisation and discourse through the 1960s and most of the 1970s. It was only in the aftermath of the Soweto uprising of 1976-77, and particularly in the years 1980-82, that the youth once again came to constitute a distinct sector of the population in terms of political mobilisation and organisation.

This is not to say that young people were politically inactive before 1980. They were, of course, central to political developments during the mid-1970s. But they were not, for the most part, organised, characterised or identified as youth. Instead they were generally referred to as students, and even as school children. There were youth clubs and self-styled national and regional youth organisations, but these were far from the core of political action among young black South Africans. Indeed, the term 'youth' was most often used politically in its apocalyptic sense, and did not denote any laudable political purpose. It was thus used to describe the unidentified participants in forms of direct action which were only tenuously linked to political struggle. As late as 1979-80, young activists, who had left school several years before, still identified themselves as students, avoiding the term 'youth'.

During 1980-82, the category of youth was reconstructed and imbued with liberatory content. The core of the new youth was the former student participants in the 1976-77 uprising, who no longer fitted into the categories of student or children and needed a new organisational home. From 1982 overtly political youth organisations or youth congresses proliferated across the country. Their concern was with politicisation and political action outside of the school and the workplace. They involved predominantly young people who had completed most, if not all, of their secondary schooling, and included students as well as ex-students.

The re-emergence or political reconstruction of the youth formed part of much broader processes of transformation in opposition politics. The most striking feature of the transformation was the rise, in the late 1970s and early 1980s, of the ANC and allied organisations from the margins to the centre of political opposition. Inside the country the presence of the ANC was felt through an expanding plethora of organisations which were covertly or implicitly allied to the banned liberation movement. These organisations often indicated their allegiances through embracing the Freedom Charter, which the ANC had adopted in 1955. The ANC-linked movement thus became known as Charterist. The emergent youth comprised an important factor propelling the growing power of the Charterist movement, which in turn shaped processes of organisation, mobilisation and definition of the youth.

Organisation in the mid-1970s

The youth of the 1980s had its origins in organisation and, above all, conflict in the mid-1970s. Young black South Africans were politicised through student organisations and youth clubs, and especially through their experiences of struggle in 1976-77. At the time, however, few young, black and politicised South Africans described themselves as youth, nor were the most prominent political or quasi-political groups referred to as youth organisations.

The most important political organisation among young black South Africans was the South African Students Organisation

(Saso). Formed by Steve Biko and others in 1969, it was one of two key organisations within the Black Consciousness movement. It organised among university students, who comprised an important but very small constituency. The role of university students in cultural and media activities gave Saso influence way beyond its limited membership.[1]

Organisation was generally weak among the very much larger numbers of secondary school students. Only in the mid-1970s did the South African Students Movement (Sasm) begin to grow significantly. It forged close links with the ANC much earlier than the more prominent Saso, from around 1973. It was Sasm activists who formed the Soweto Students Representative Council, which played a key role in the events of June 1976 and the following months.[2]

Organisationally, Saso and Sasm may have had a limited reach. But they responded to increasingly assertive student cultures. The ideas of Black Consciousness had a broader impact than Black Consciousness organisations themselves, and were fueled by political developments in the region. Students were highly aware of the independence of Mozambique and Angola in 1975, the failure of direct South African military intervention in Angola, and the escalation of armed struggle in Rhodesia.

Saso and Sasm organised the small number of highly politicised young students. A much wider range of students, and to a lesser extent other young urban people, were involved in youth groups and clubs. These generally organised sporting and social activities; many were linked to churches. Youth clubs engaged in cultural activities such as poetry readings and drama productions, and in community work, all of which could serve as politicising events. Many also engaged in political debate, either formally or informally. A few drew young people into more active politics linked to the banned liberation movements.

---

1 On Saso, see Hirson, B: *Year of Fire, Year of Ash: the Soweto revolt* (London: Zed, 1979); Brooks, A and Brickhill, J: *Whirlwind Before the Storm* (London: International Defence and Aid Fund, 1980).
2 Diseko, N: 'The origins and development of the South African Students Movement', *Journal of Southern African Studies* 18/1 (March 1992); Brooks and Brickhill: *Whirlwind*, pp. 85-95.

The youth re-emerge, 1976-84

The Esukhayeni Youth Club in Soweto, for example, had over a hundred members in 1975, of which about seventy were paid-up. Some of its members were active in Sasm. In a series of trials in 1975-77, the state alleged that the club was a front for pro-ANC activity. The club's leading members included Tieho Masinga (acquitted of terrorism in 1977) and Amos Masondo (convicted of terrorism in 1976).[3] Another club which became prominent in media reports was the Young African Christian Movement in Kagiso on the West Rand. This was an inter-denominational youth club with the ostensible purpose of keeping young people away from drinking, 'delinquency and hooliganism', and promoting sporting, religious and community-oriented activity. According to the state, however, it was a front for the Pan-Africanist Congress (PAC).[4]

Youth clubs at the local level played an important role in exposing young people to political ideas. Many of them were run by ex-students, especially former members of Saso, who emphasised drama and other cultural activities as methods of raising political consciousness. This strategy was clearly informed by a Black Consciousness perspective, but was often also sympathetic to, and even oriented to, the ANC (or sometimes the PAC). Such youth clubs were not only formed in the major townships, but also in smaller ones. In Tumahole, in the northern Orange Free State, for example, the Parys African Students Organisation was formed in 1975. Its founders (led by a student from Fort Hare) sought to 'conscientise' students and ex-students through performing semi-political plays. For example, a play on crime 'tried to show that the crime is not just because one does it, but because of oppression and exploitation'.[5]

Raising political issues was often contentious in these semi-political youth clubs. This was in part due to the context of repression and vulnerability at the time, but also because of resistance

---

3 See evidence of Masinga, *State vs Sexwale and 11 others*; also Moss, G: *Political Trials in South Africa* (Johannesburg: Development Studies Group 1979).
4 See evidence in *State vs Mothopeng and 17 others*, of Hlatswayo, Matsobane, Nyathi, Sehume, Sompondo, Sejanamane, etc.
5 Interview, F Dabi, Vereeniging, January 1986. See also Seekings, J: 'Political Mobilisation in Tumahole, 1984-85', *Africa Perspective* 7/8 (October 1989), pp. 111-114.

from general membership to activists seen as imposing their own political agenda. The Parys African Students Organisation, for example, collapsed because of disagreement over how political the plays should be, and how involved the club should become in community issues.

Ex-students often remained involved in these local level youth clubs after leaving school. At the regional and national level, several 'youth' organisations were formed in the mid-1970s to provide a home for ex-student activists. These included the National Youth Organisation (Nayo) and the Transvaal Youth Organisation. While these remain largely unresearched, it seems that their impact was limited. According to Brooks and Brickhill,

> *Despite its name and intentions, Nayo did not manage to become a national youth movement. At best it was a loose confederation of regional or local groupings of young militants in some of the main urban areas.*[6]

Nayo and the regional organisations were closely linked to Sasm, and were ANC-oriented; their main concern may have been recruitment for the ANC and its armed wing, Umkhonto we Sizwe. Their direct influence was especially curtailed when they were hit by detentions and trials in 1975-76.

In October 1977 Saso, Sasm, Nayo and the regional youth organisations were banned. Many of their leading members were imprisoned, detained or left the country. Later, former Sasm members were to play an important role in the development of student and youth organisation. Some of the more politicised local youth clubs also folded in the aftermath of 1976, but others endured or were established, continuing to politicise young people and create new generations of activists.

The uprisings of 1976-77

Student organisations and youth clubs played an important role in the politicisation of a core of young black South Africans in the

---

6   Brooks and Brickhill: *Whirlwind*, pp. 80-85.

mid-1970s. But the uprisings of 1976-77 mobilised and politicised much larger numbers of people, as well as reviving a tradition of defiance and protest. The events of 1976-77 have been well-documented elsewhere, and will not be examined here.[7] It is appropriate, however, to consider briefly who took part in the protest, and in particular which young people participated and how the category of youth was understood at the time.

The social composition of the protesters in 1976-77 has been inadequately explored in existing accounts. There seem to be three reasons for this. Firstly, the uprising was initially a student protest, and it was often assumed that the participants in all the events – including riots – were students. Secondly, the studies draw on a limited range of sources, with little use of oral testimony or even court records. These accounts therefore view the revolt from the outside, focusing on the 'objective' features of the structural context rather than on the participants. Thirdly, writing about 1976 was itself a politically important task. This strongly influenced the identification of participants in the conflict.

How protesters were identified and described affected the way in which the revolt was understood, and which responses were appropriate. Sympathetic observers saw protesters acting with restraint and good reason, or as the supposed repositories of the revolutionary mission, selflessly performing their roles. The state and other conservative commentators, unable to portray the township protests and conflicts in terms of tribal animosities, sought to criminalise them through attributing them to rampaging and self-serving *tsotsis* (often externally manipulated); the 'problem' was thus primarily one of law and order. As a result, the identity of the protesters was contested.

Molteno, in a review of the early literature of 1976, condemns the heavily loaded and pervasive 'ruling class terminology' at length. He writes of one study (written by a former colonial policeman, Hitchcock):

---

7   See Hirson: *Year of Fire*; Brooks and Brickhill: *Whirlwind*; Kane-Berman, J: *Soweto: Black Revolt, White Reaction* (Johannesburg: Ravan, 1978); Report of the Commission of Inquiry into the Riots of Soweto and Elsewhere (the Cillie Commission).

> *Making it seem as though the violence that ensued was initiated by these pupils and as though things were taken over by criminal and degenerate elements, Hitchcock writes that 'Within minutes of the first stones being thrown, the students ... were joined by hundreds of Soweto's roughnecks. Among them were big-time bandits, tsotsis, drug addicts, drunkards and won't-works'. The 'rioters' were soon, amongst other things, looting bottle-stores 'for hard liquor'. By the next day, 'the angry drunken mobs were armed with pick-axes, iron bars, shovels, sticks and the inevitable stones and half-bricks'.*[8]

This terminology and perspective was not confined to the more reactionary tracts. Molteno condemns the liberal South African Institute of Race Relations for describing 'mobs' going 'on the rampage', with rioting on 17 June 1976, 'apparently now led by *tsotsis* and gangsters who had taken advantage of the previous day's violence and had started looting'.

But such terminology was so widespread because this kind of description was not entirely false. It was a half-truth. Students and 'respectable' adults were central to the protests, undoubtedly also participating in arson and looting. But they were joined in such protests by a range of other residents. Furthermore, few students were as clearly 'politically' motivated as the student leadership. Some studies have obscured this. Thus, in Hirson's account, *students* gathered to protest on 16 June, marched with placards, and were shot at by police. But by 10 am, the demonstrating students had become the *youth*, 'surging through Soweto', killing, looting, stoning and burning.

Hirson does not indicate who comprised this 'youth', although he does write that the crowd was 'an ever changing mass of people' who would sometimes 'metamorphose into a seething, furious mass that sought revenge', and it later seems that unemployed people were involved.[9] Brooks and Brickhill in general portray a curiously homogeneous 'community'. They do indicate that *tsotsis* 'played an ambiguous role in the uprising, at times exploiting situ-

---

8 Molteno, F: 'The Uprising of 16 June: a review of the literature on events in South Africa 1976', *Social Dynamics* 5/1 (1979), pp. 58-9.
9 Molteno: 'The Uprising of 16 June', pp. 60-61, quoting *Race Relations Survey 1976*, p. 72.

ations to loot, rob and extort, at other times joining in with the students in the battle against their common foe, the police.'[10]

Molteno's reaction to the portrayal of protesters as self-serving *tsotsis* arose in part out of a reasonable concern to avoid denigrating and delegitimating what were seen as, for the most part, quite reasonable protests that required socio-economic and political solutions, not repression. But identifying *tsotsis* in the crowds, or students with more ambiguous motives, does not mean accepting Hitchcock's fears and biases. Looting, arson and killing can be ordered and rational; even responsible students can be brutal; and a wide range of people may participate in riots. Similarly, incidents of violence (or looting) need not detract from the justice of the main grievances and protests.

The question remains: who was involved, in which protests or events, and at which times? Detailed answers must await local histories and autobiographical accounts of these events, but Kane-Berman provides some general figures as regards the ages of participants. The ages of 1 200 presumed participants were collated using press reports of people killed or injured, admitted to hospital or brought to court. Forty-four per cent were aged thirteen to sixteen; forty-nine per cent between seventeen and twenty-three; and seven per cent were twenty-four or over. But just over one-third of the people killed were aged over twenty-six, and only a quarter or so were under eighteen, according to some estimates. Data in the Cillie Report suggests that about a quarter of the people killed on the Reef were aged thirty-two or over; about forty per cent were aged twenty or under. These figures indicate a surprisingly high incidence of older people among the fatalities (although it must be remembered that there were sizable numbers of older students; the average age of matric students in 1973 was nineteen).[11]

More important than age is the ill-defined division between students and the non-student youth (the 'push-outs', as they were sometimes called). There are unfortunately no anthropological or sociological studies of gangs and their activities in Soweto and other African townships at this time. There were certainly many

---

10 Brooks and Brickhill: *Whirlwind*, p. 151.
11 Kane-Berman: *Soweto*, pp. 7-8.

young unemployed people outside the schools, even before the class and school boycotts. Crudely estimated, there were probably as many out-of-work and out-of-school youths in their late teens and early twenties as were in the schools. But few of these were active in professional gangs. Such gangs do not seem to have been as prominent in African townships in the 1970s as they had been in the 1950s, or still were in coloured townships. Most 'gangs' were simply unarmed township kids (including school students) organised by locality as social rather than full-time activities.[12]

Non-students should not be ignored, however. The novelist Mbulelo Mzamane describes the professional 'Hazel' gang participating in the looting of beerhalls and bottlestores. Its members arrived, 'already prepared with petrol cans, empty cardboard boxes and a truck, the moment our boys approached the bottlestore'. Here was a clear case of profiteering, with the looted liquor finding its way to shebeens. Later on Mzamane writes that thefts from white traders escalated and the gangs redistributed the stolen goods in the townships:

> *Gangs of petty thieves, trouble-shooters and small-time tsotsis, who spent their leisure-time staff-riding on the trains or lounging aimlessly around the shops, spinning unlikely yarns about improbable acts, were suddenly moved by a crusading spirit, inspired with lofty ideals and fired with a new zeal ... For the social lepers of Soweto, a flame of charity burning brightly in their bosoms, it was a glorious game ... Theft without its customary stigma ... What could be more absolving and gratifying than this new discovery of the saving graces of crime, of the notion of crime as a means of social rehabilitation?*

Mzamane describes the gangs as gripped by a 'truly altruistic spirit'. But action was also, as Mzamane puts it, a 'glorious game', and the game no doubt provided material gains as well.[13]

---

12   Interviews, Kagiso and Soweto, 1989-90.
13   Mzamane, M: *The Children of Soweto* (London: Longman, 1982), pp. 112, 149-150. There is not even a hint of irony in Mzamane's account.

The youth re-emerge, 1976-84

Students themselves were not a monolithic category, nor were they motivated by educational or political grievances alone. In Kagiso, higher primary school students who participated in some of the early incidents remember it primarily in terms of 'fun'. One recalled the attack on the beerhall because it was the first time he had ever tasted beer; when he took it home his father was very angry, beat him and hid the beer in the yard, drinking it surreptitiously later.[14] Looting was in anybody's material interests, students included. Students and student leaders were sometimes also divided over tactical questions such as whether class boycotts should be continued and examinations written. Strong support for a return to school in the second half of July 1976 was undoubtedly one factor in the proliferation of arson attacks on schools: the arsonists included students who wanted to prevent a return to class.

The impact of 1976 on youth politics

The uprisings of 1976-77 were crushed through a combination of severe repression, detentions and bannings, flight into exile, and the accumulating weaknesses of the residual student-based leadership. But the events were to have a profound impact on opposition politics. First, the uprisings not only provoked a revitalisation of the ANC, but more specifically focused its attention on the political potential of internal organisation in general, and of the youth in particular.

The ANC enjoyed a huge influx of fleeing students. In 1978-79 a rethink of ANC strategy led to an increased emphasis on working with and through semi-legal or legal organisations inside the country.[15] The ANC thus linked up with those activists who stayed inside the country, building up organisation.

Secondly, there was an organisational vacuum inside the country for almost two years after the banning of student and other political organisations in 1977. The Black Consciousness move-

---

14 Interviews, 1989.
15 Barrell, H: 'The Turn to the Masses: the African National Congress Strategic Review of 1978-9', *Journal of Southern African Studies* 18/1 (March 1992).

ment, which had been the primary target of the bannings, never fully recovered. Instead it was ANC-aligned or Charterist organisations and activists which came to dominate the mainstream of internal resistance. From 1979 a series of Charterist organisations was formed and Charterist activists gained control over non-Charterist organisations. Emphasising action, the Charterist movement initiated or took over a series of campaigns and events. The profile of the ANC and the Freedom Charter grew. In 1983-84 a flurry of organisational development and protest was centered around the formation of the United Democratic Front (UDF). This marked Charterist domination of the deepening political opposition to the state.

The development of youth organisation was also shaped by the ways in which the experiences of 1976 were theorised in exile, on Robben Island and elsewhere inside the country. Students and former students were identified as an important constituency, but one which needed organisation, political direction and education. The belief among students that they could serve as a political vanguard was diagnosed as mistaken. The student-based leadership of 1976 was seen with hindsight to have been organisationally inexperienced, and arrogant in its dealings with 'workers' and 'parents', who were dismissed as unpoliticised. Students and especially former students would henceforth be encouraged to develop organisation among workers and older people.[16] The 'graduates' of 1976, ie the students who had protested, fought and hence 'graduated' in the uprising, were to play a prominent role in civic organisations and trade unions, as well as youth organisations, in the early 1980s.

Thirdly, the revolt shaped the attitudes of thousands of young people, nurturing widespread defiance of authority. Lunn quotes an interviewee who stated:

Before '76 most schoolgoing children were controlled. OK, even they had drinking sessions, or whatever, they did try to hide it from their parents. '76 brought a new breed of schoolgoing kids. You find that now even immediately after '76 children would not be bothered being seen in their school uniforms in

---

16 Interviews with M Morobe, O Monareng, Johannesburg, April 1992.

shebeens. They were more open and more defiant and more politically aware than the pre-'76 era.[17]

The militant young activists were clearly not children anymore, and few remained students for very long.

The radicalisation of attitudes to some extent acted against the view that broad-based organisation needed to be developed. Radicalisation often involved an emphasis on immediate, militarist solutions. It was only during the following years of slow and difficult struggle that many ex-student activists recognised the importance of responsive organisation rather than just mobilisation.

Finally, the state's responses to the 1976-77 uprisings provided conditions in which student militancy was to rise, not fall. As we saw above, the state's expansion of the secondary school system generated new grievances and fostered a highly militant section of the population.

Youth in 'student' organisation, 1979-82

Among the first of the new Charterist organisations to emerge – and certainly the first to align openly with the ANC – was the Congress of South African Students (Cosas), formed in 1979. Despite its name, Cosas branches provided an organisational home for many non-student youth until 1982, when the organisation decided that membership should be limited to school students. Between 1979 and 1982 Cosas leaders repeatedly debated the scope of student organisation, grappling with their identity. The history of Cosas thus straddles the period in which the category of youth was reconstructed to embrace politicised former student activists.[18]

---

17 Quoted by Lunn, H: 'Antecedents of the Music and Popular Culture of the African Post-1976 Generation', unpublished MA dissertation, University of the Witwatersrand, (1986), p. 233.
18 This section is based on Matona: 'Student Organisation'; Diseko: 'Education struggle'; and interviews with M Mditshwa, N Mogase, S Moloi, O Monareng, J Ngwenya, M Nkomfe and M Scott.

Cosas was formed in June 1979 by Transvaal-based ex-Sasm leaders and students who had emerged during the events of 1976-77. Oriented towards the ANC, the group was concerned to maintain the momentum of the student-led resistance of 1976-77. Initially they had wanted to form a broad political organisation, but were persuaded to establish a body ostensibly for students. However, few of these leaders were still students, and Cosas remained dominated by ex-students until 1982. During this time Cosas served more as a general youth organisation (with close contact with the ANC in exile) than a student-based structure, and rarely took up school-related issues.

The ambiguity over the range of Cosas's membership and constituency gave rise to debate and discussion from the outset. At the founding conference, a four-person 'Youth Co-ordinating Committee' was appointed to look into the organisation of students in tertiary education as well as of young people who were not studying. The committee was hampered by lack of resources, which prevented easy travel, and by an absence of direction and urgency.

There was no agreement over which groups of young people should be organised by Cosas. Some activists believed that Cosas should grow into a body uniting all students, at whatever level. But the dominant view at the inaugural conference was that Cosas should not organise students in tertiary education. The issue was unexpectedly resolved when a separate and rival organisation was set up to organise in the tertiary educational sector. The Azanian Students Organisation (Azaso) was formed by the Azanian People's Organisation (Azapo), which was hostile to the ANC and the nascent Charterist movement inside the country. According to one Cosas activist, 'Azapo beat us to it'.[19] Pro-Charterist students decided to seize control of Azaso rather than outflank it. They achieved this objective at an Azaso annual congress in June 1981, but the division between secondary and tertiary level students remained.

A more difficult problem was the inclusion of non-school going youth. The issue here was not so much school drop-outs, who were largely disregarded, but students who had completed their

---
Johannesburg and Durban, 1992.
19 Interview, Mditshwa.

schooling but not continued in higher education. Although Cosas was established at a time when schooling was returning to normal after the events of 1976-77, most of its leading founders were ex-students rather than students. For example, Cosas Eastern Cape co-ordinator, Monde Mditshwa, had left school two years earlier, in mid-1977. Cosas readily accommodated young people who had left school but, having never worked, still regarded themselves as students. For example, Petrus Malindi was re-elected to the executive committee of the Vaal Triangle Cosas branch after he ceased to be even a part-time student. He explained this in the following way:

> That was because I had not yet taken a decision of [sic] leaving school altogether. During the years 1981 and 1982 I was still considering myself a learner, because I was reading during that period and because I still had interest in school affairs. That is why I considered myself to be still a student.[20]

The involvement of ex-students was unproblematic as long as Cosas defined itself primarily in terms of political rather than educational struggle. Cosas seemed to be developing well, and there was thus no urgency about forming a separate youth movement.

Changing conditions in 1980-81 revived the issue. First, a wave of student protests in 1980 threw up a new generation of leadership in Cosas, and emphasised the importance of engaging with school students over school-based grievances. Cosas leaders began to realise that it was difficult for non-students to organise in the classroom. In the Western Cape, school boycotts in coloured schools radicalised large numbers of students who subsequently became involved in local youth organisations. In the Eastern Cape, school protests in African schools created leaders who moved into Cosas. Although the entire initial Cosas leadership had come from the Transvaal, all three presidents in office from 1980 to 1984 (Zenzile, Mati and Johnson) came from the Eastern Cape.

Secondly, Cosas leaders experienced constant police harassment. The initial executive was detained in late 1979, and in the following year the first president (Eph Mogale) was convicted of

---

20 Evidence in *State vs Baleka and others*, pp. 10741-2.

furthering the aims of a banned organisation (the ANC). In 1980 police detained Cosas leaders across the country in apparent preparation for a major trial. The detainees were released when it emerged that the police had insufficient evidence. The police seemed to believe that Cosas was primarily a front for the ANC, and was recruiting for the ANC's armed wing, Umkhonto we Sizwe (MK). When Cosas leaders under interrogation protested that it was a student organisation, police asked why its leaders were not students. Charterist leaders believed that redirecting Cosas toward students and educational grievances would reduce police harassment.

In addition, advice came from Robben Island and exile that activists needed to organise the youth outside schools. The influx of ex-students into the ANC in exile raised the issue of non-student youth within the liberation movement. In 1980 the ANC began to refer to 'the youth' rather than students, and it declared 1981 to be the 'year of the youth'.[21] ANC leader Oscar Mpetha later said that Robben Island prisoners

had decided that the key to success lay in organisation of the youth. History has shown that there would be no freedom without the youth being properly organised and encouraged to play their rightful role.'[22]

Political prisoners released from Robben Island conveyed the message that youth congresses should be formed.

This process culminated in a decision at Cosas' May 1982 conference to limit membership to school students, and to assist the formation of separate youth structures for ex-students. Soon after this, in August, the ANC convened its first youth conference, held in Tanzania.

The theme of the conference was 'the role of the youth in the liberation struggle'. Curiously, ANC president Oliver Tambo, in his address to the conference, did not mention the need for distinct youth organisation. Instead he urged the working youth to become involved in trade unions, students in student organisation, and

---

21 *Sechaba*, (March 1981). See also *Sechaba*: 'Youth and the Freedom Charter', (April 1981).
22 *Saspu National* 4/3 (September 1983).

other youth to join MK.[23] This may have reflected a continued belief that separate youth structures were seen primarily as recruitment agencies for MK.

Ex-students who had been active in Cosas now needed to find new organisational homes. Younger militants in this residual category were discouraged from involvement in civic organisations, which were intended to be organisations of household heads and other, older, township residents. They were also formed to take up civic issues rather than explicitly political ones. In the absence of a political party, new organisations were required, and youth congresses began to fill this need.

During the period 1979-82, many youth were active through supposedly student organisation. The limits of student organisation reflected and imposed parameters on the organisation of the youth. The strength of Cosas was concentrated in African townships, firstly in the PWV region and from 1980 in the Eastern Cape. Cosas remained relatively weak in African townships in both Natal and the Western Cape. Furthermore, Cosas had very little presence in coloured or Indian schools. Even after the widespread school boycotts of 1980, Cosas failed to move into these areas, while very few coloured and Indian student activists moved into Cosas after leaving school.

National youth organisation, 1982-84

From 1982 to 1984 there was broad agreement over the differences between youth and student organisation, even if in practice there was some overlap in membership. The category of youth included politically conscious young people who were politically active outside of the workplace and school. During this period tentative moves continued towards the formation of a national youth organisation within the Charterist movement. Although such an organisation was not formed until much later, regional and national networks of youth activists did cohere. These informal youth networks operated within the broader and fast-growing Charterist

---

23 *Sechaba*, (October 1982).

political networks. Many local youth groupings were thus linked with each other through the ANC underground, or through clandestine ANC-oriented study groups.[24]

Youth activists were also involved (with other activists) in the committees set up to co-ordinate specific campaigns. In 1981, for example, campaigns were conducted in protest against Republic Day, Ciskei's 'independence', and elections to the South African Indian Council, as well as in support of striking workers at Wilson-Rowntree. Such campaigns played an important role in raising political consciousness and promoting youth organisation at local, regional and national levels.

The task of preparing formal national and local youth organisation was entrusted to a committee appointed at the 1982 Cosas conference. This committee included ex-student activists from Soweto, Port Elizabeth and elsewhere. The committee decided that local structures should be developed prior to forming a national organisation, so that local structures should not be seen as imposed 'from above'. But, like its predecessor appointed in 1979, the committee lacked resources. This situation was improved when Deacon Mathe (a former Robben Islander from Atteridgeville, outside Pretoria) was seconded to the committee by his employer, the Johannesburg-based Community Research and Information Centre (Cric). But the development of national youth organisation remained bedeviled by deepening disunity among youth activists.

From mid-1983 the United Democratic Front provided some national and regional co-ordination of youth groups. The UDF was formed in order to co-ordinate internal opposition to apartheid, and specifically to the tri-cameral parliament and certain legislation. Nationally, the UDF held conferences in August and December 1983, and in each region representatives of the UDF's affiliates regularly met in general council meetings. Most regions also had a youth representative on the regional executive committee. Ironically, perhaps, many youth activists were distracted from building youth organisation through their involvement in the preparation for and formation of the UDF, and in its early campaigns. Thus, while some progress was made in developing local structures and

---

24 This section is based on interviews with B Dlamini, P Mashatile, P Mokaba, O Monareng, M Nkomfe and S Ntombela.

national networks, very little progress was made towards a formal national body.

In January 1984 a youth conference was held at Wilgespruit on the West Rand to assess the call for a national youth organisation. The existing steering committee was revamped, with new members including Rapu Molekane (of the Young Christian Students, from Soweto), Paul Mashatile (president of the Alexandra Youth Congress) and Dan Montsisi (former Robben Islander, from Soweto). Deacon Mathe co-ordinated the committee, which – like its predecessors – made slow progress. This was in part due to activists' involvement in national political campaigns and, in the Transvaal, escalating protests and confrontations in the second half of 1984.

Towards the end of 1984 older activists from the UDF and South African Council of Churches suggested that youth organisations should campaign during 1985 around the International Youth Year (IYY) called by the United Nations. The IYY would serve as a focus for highly politicised youth groups to work with less politicised groups, thereby building a youth front (similar to the UDF itself) which could then grow into a national youth structure. In November 1984 a national meeting of Charterist youth activists, including representatives from Indian and coloured areas, was held in Lenasia to plan campaigns around International Youth Year. A further conference was held in January 1985 south of Durban (at Mnani Camp).

At both of these meetings, and in the following year, activity was almost paralysed by disagreement between two different political groupings. Both of these groups were Charterist or ANC-aligned (rival Black Consciousness or other youth groups did not participate in these 'national' meetings). The Durban conference elected a committee to continue to plan the formation of a national youth organisation, convened by Mathe. The campaign around IYY was organised separately, however, by a national co-ordinator (Montsisi) and a committee.

Local youth organisation and protest, 1980-84

The early 1980s saw the formation of a range of youth organisations at the local level. A number of forms of organisation can be distinguished, besides the local 'student' structures considered above:

☆ several short-lived 'youth' groupings were formed in 1980-81, essentially to recruit for Umkhonto we Sizwe;
☆ longer lasting youth organisations, in African as well as Indian and coloured areas, were by-and-large less overtly political. These included branches of religious organisations such as Young Christian Workers (YCW) or Young Christian Students (YCS), as well as locally-based groups;
☆ following the 1982 Cosas decision, a series of overtly political youth congresses or organisations were formed.

As in the 1970s, many political youth organisations and Cosas branches drew members and leaders from localised youth clubs. These clubs continued to provide an important forum for the politicisation of students and other youth in the late 1970s and early 1980s. The YCW and YCS also provided an important channel through which young people were politicised. Many prominent student or youth activists passed through one or other of these organisations. YCW and YCS branches received support from their national structures, while other local semi-political youth groups tended to rely on the support or dynamism of individual patrons or members.

In the West Rand township of Kagiso, for example, four semi-political youth groups operated in the early 1980s. The first was based around Frank Chikane, who was later to become prominent as general-secretary of the South African Council of Churches, but was then the local Apostolic Faith Mission priest. Chikane was also closely involved in the growing Charterist network on the Reef. In 1978 several church-linked youth groups came together under Chikane's patronage to form an Inter-denominational Youth

Christian Club (IYCC), which engaged in social as well as religious activity. It ran welfare projects, assisted in the local advice office, and conducted a household survey in the township to identify residents' major problems.

The second of Kagiso's semi-political youth organisations was also church-based. A local branch of the Young Christian Workers (YCW) served as a semi-political youth club. YCW members played a leading role in the formation of the local civic in 1981, with one member serving as the civic's first secretary. Members of both the IYCC and YCW were active in the third local grouping, a branch of Cosas. Finally, there was a branch of Azanyu, formed nationally in 1981 as the Black Consciousness-oriented alternative to Cosas. The Kagiso branch was formed in early 1982, but suffered from state harassment and failed to attract much support.[25]

A similar range of youth organisations was formed in many townships as well as in coloured and Indian areas. It proved, however, very difficult to forge links across the divide of separate group areas. The development of youth organisation was hindered and shaped by apartheid's 'racial' divisions. The racially segregated education system was important in maintaining these divisions. Faced with different educational authorities and grievances, and inheriting different political traditions, students and ex-students organised into separate structures. Cosas had served as a political home for many former students from African townships, but rarely for their coloured and Indian counterparts (and never, of course, for white students).

The weakness of Cosas in coloured and Indian areas ironically underlay the relative strength of independent youth organisation in some of those areas, especially in coloured areas in Cape Town but to a lesser extent in coloured and Indian areas on the Reef and Durban.

There were regional differences in the strength of Charterist youth organisations over and above the racial factor. Attitude surveys conducted in 1985 showed that there was little awareness of Cosas and the more overtly politicised youth organisations in Cape

---

25 On the IYCC, YCW and Cosas, see interviews with L Ntlokoa, T Moiloa, G Moiloa, B Ntsamane, B Seripe and I Genu, Johannesburg and Kagiso, 1989-90.

Town and Durban; cultural youth organisations were much stronger.[26]

Youth organisations were strong and active in coloured areas of the Western Cape. The 1980 school boycotts swept through coloured schools, and many students came into contact with older, more overtly political, activists. Many of the leaders of the boycotts, and other students, moved into youth organisations after leaving school. These 1980 student activists thus contrasted with their 1976-77 predecessors, many of whom went into exile. The resultant youth groups included the Mitchells Plain Youth Movement (which itself had six branches from 1981-82), the Lansdowne Youth Movement and the Hanover Park Youth Wing (constituted as the 'wing' of the local civic organisation). These came together in 1983 in the Cape Youth Congress (Cayco), which was formed with thirty-eight branches (although some existed only in name). In contrast to other youth congresses established at about the same time, Cayco was formed out of existing youth organisations rather than by youth shifting out of 'student' structures.[27]

There were at this time no political or semi-political youth organisations in Cape Town's African areas. A small number of youth were involved in Cosas, and otherwise there were poetry, jazz and sports groups. The only contact between coloured and African youth was through church groups such as YCW and YCS. Prior to the formation of Cayco, coloured student leaders sought to draw in African youth. While some African youth did attend the launch, and some were elected onto the executive, Cayco remained an essentially coloured youth grouping until 1985-86. Indeed, some of the African youth who served as additional members of Cayco's first executive committee in effect withdrew because of disagreements between them and the coloured youth leadership. Rose Sonto – from an African township – was elected as Cayco's second president in a clear attempt to promote a more inclusive image for the organisation.[28]

---

26 Meer, F (ed): *The Power of the Powerless: a study of South Africa's disenfranchised* (Durban: Madiba Publications, 1991), p. 112.
27 Interviews: L Wort and T Oosterwyk.
28 Interviews: Wort, Oosterwyk, Sonto.

On the Reef, there were youth organisations in the coloured areas of Reiger Park and Bosmont, and in the Indian areas of Lenasia and in Benoni, but these were much weaker than their Cape counterparts.

In Durban, youth organisation in Indian and African areas also developed in parallel rather than together. Following the 1980 school boycotts, Indian student activists formed Helping Hands to organise social and charitable activities. Participation in Helping Hands politicised many younger Indian students and youth.[29]

In Durban's African areas, student and youth organisation was weak. The exception to this was Lamontville, where the Masibosane Lamontville Youth Organisation (Malayo) drew young activists into civic and political work.[30] There were two comparable youth groups in Pietermaritzburg's African townships. The DCO Matiwane Youth League, formed in 1980, met at the Edendale Ecumenical Lay Centre, where its leading member was employed as a youth organiser. The League organised social activities as well as providing a forum for political discussion. It attracted members – mostly students – from Pietermaritzburg's other townships, and in 1982 some of its members from Sobantu formed a separate Sobantu Youth League.[31]

These youth organisations varied in terms of how explicitly political they were. Church-based groups, and the youth organisations in coloured areas of the Western Cape, generally provided a range of religious or social activities, with the political content being less overt. A few local youth organisations were, by contrast, primarily concerned with political issues, and even recruitment for MK. Such organisations rarely survived police attention, and arrests and convictions rapidly depleted both leadership and membership. The short-lived KwaMashu-based African Youth Congress in Durban around 1980 seems to have been one example of this.[32] Internal, non-violent organisation and action was still less attractive than the lure of MK and the armed struggle.

---

29 Naidoo: 'The Politics of Youth Resistance'; see also Julie Frederikse's interview with Kumi Naidoo (in the Popular History Trust collection held at the South African Historical Archives in Johannesburg).
30 Interviews: L Tsenoli, J Sithole and B Dlamini.
31 Interviews: M Ndlovu, M Wittenberg.
32 Interviews: S Ntombela, P Mokaba.

Following the 1982 Cosas conference, ex-Cosas activists joined with recently-released political prisoners in forming further, explicitly political, youth congresses. The most prominent of these were the Soweto, Alexandra and Port Elizabeth Youth Congresses (Soyco, Ayco and Peyco), together with the Saulsville-Atteridgeville and Mamelodi Youth Organisations (Sayo and Mayo, both from Pretoria). Less prominent examples included youth congresses in Uitenhage, Mangaung (Bloemfontein), and Mankweng (Pietersburg), the KwaMashu Youth League, and the Tumahole Students Organisation (which, like its predecessors, was not primarily a student organisation at all). In many other areas, less formal groups cohered. In the Vaal Triangle, for example, ex-Cosas activists formed a committee which met fairly regularly, and even took minutes. The group was not very active, however, and was not formally launched.[33] These youth organisations were brought together with more established ANC-oriented organisations in the UDF, launched nationally in August 1983.

The new youth congresses formed in 1983 were, unlike most of their predecessors, overtly political. This posed severe organisational problems in terms of the meaning of 'political'. Most youth congresses were formed amidst severe factional conflict as rival groups of activists struggled to ensure that their particular ideological or organisational perspective predominated within the new structure. The process of forming the Alexandra Youth Congress illustrates this, where two sets of politicised youth were grouped around the 'workerist' Ditshwantsho tsa Rona, which produced a township newsletter, and Cosas. The youth differed over whether the prospective youth congress should adopt the Freedom Charter, and over elections to the steering committee. The ex-Cosas grouping held a majority, voted themselves into office and adopted the Freedom Charter. The defeated grouping withdrew from the youth congress.[34]

In Cape Town, Cayco's formation was also dominated by factional divisions and, eventually, a caucused compromise.[35] The

33 Malindi evidence, *State vs Baleka and others*.
34 Carter, C: '"We are the progressives": Alexandra Youth Congress activists and the Freedom Charter, 1983-85', *Journal of Southern African Studies* 17/2 (June 1991).
35 Interviews: Wort and Oosterwyk.

The youth re-emerge, 1976-84

East London Youth Congress was torn apart by factional struggles, and at one stage even disaffiliated from the UDF. During 1984-85, as will be seen below, deep divisions were to weaken youth organisation across the country.

Notwithstanding these tensions and struggles, the 'political', and indeed Charterist, character of the youth congresses was clear from the outset. At the various launches, veteran Charterist leaders spoke, freedom songs were sung and Charterist symbolism was pervasive. This was also reflected in the importance attached to the Freedom Charter itself. Carter writes that in Alexandra, the Freedom Charter

> *offered a symbolic, and for some a real, link to the ANC; in the context of Alexandra's metropolitan setting, embracing the Freedom Charter and the UDF meant in the most practical sense easy access to other political activists, who in turn provided organisational resources and a sense of solidarity; and the document became in the hands of some youth activists a creed for the purposes of recruitment and political conscientisation.*[36]

Banned ANC literature, as well as tape recordings of Radio Freedom broadcasts, were widely circulated among the members of these youth organisations.

While the youth organisations formed in 1983-84 were generally more overtly political than their predecessors, there were exceptions. In areas where there were few politicised students coming out of Cosas or existing youth groups (for example, in coloured areas of the Western Cape), new youth groups adopted less of a political profile. To have done otherwise would have precluded the drawing in of significant numbers of youth.

In Durban, an umbrella Youth Forum was established under the auspices of Diakonia (a Christian centre) in 1983. The Youth Forum brought together new and more political groupings such as the KwaMashu Youth League, older and established groups such as Malayo (from Lamontville) and Helping Hands (from Chatsworth), as well as church-based and other groups which remained wary of direct political involvement.[37]

---

36 Carter: 'Alexandra Youth'.

The dangers of political activity in areas where there were few politicised activists is well illustrated in the experience of the DCO Matiwane Youth League in Edendale. Having drawn in, and politicised, youth from all over Pietermaritzburg, the League collapsed when the police raided its meeting place and found ammunition; the League's organiser was arrested, tried and convicted. Many members were deterred, and the League ground to a standstill.[38]

Prior to the township revolt of the mid-1980s, the membership of youth congresses included predominantly school students, older students and recent school-leavers (whether young workers or unemployed). There was often considerable overlap between the membership of the youth congress and local Cosas branches, with some students in both. The unifying factor was a self-conscious commitment to liberation, and enthusiasm for political action within the township rather than school or workplace.

The members of these youth organisations were almost all well-educated in the sense of having completed most or all of their secondary schooling. The DCO Matiwane Youth League, for example, was made up mostly of well-educated children of professional people. Their discussions were held in English. The League was locally regarded as elitist and unaccommodating. Most of these organisations had a small membership. The usual attendance at DCO Matiwane meetings was about fifty.[39]

It is unclear whether the composition of the DCO Matiwane Youth League was typical, but there is evidence that most youth congresses at this time were comprised mainly of better-schooled people. The forms of political education undertaken within youth congresses sometimes reinforced this pattern.

The composition of the active youth inside the country during this period was reflected in the content of the ANC's January 1985 anniversary statement. The ANC saluted working youth and students, who had earned the title of 'young lions'. Unemployed youth were still not mentioned.[40]

---

37 See Naidoo: 'Politics of youth resistance'.
38 Interview: M Ndlovu.
39 Interview: Ndlovu.
40 *Sechaba*, (March 1985).

For several reasons youth organisations generally maintained a low political profile in this period. Not only were there few youth organisations and activists (especially in comparison with later periods), but they often consciously steered clear of overtly political activities. By avoiding being seen as political, they hoped to reduce police harassment and attract a wider range of potential participants. Individual youth activists, however, often played central roles in broader campaigns such as the 1981 Anti-Republic Day struggle. At the local level young people were involved in civic struggles, such as protests against rent increases.

During this period, protests drew in small numbers of young people in comparison with the subsequent period. Participation was generally limited to the active and intellectually politicised membership of political youth groups. Less well-educated young people, more junior students, unemployed people and gangs seem to have stayed away.

Some protests, however created conditions which other young people were able to use to their advantage. This was the case with the widespread school boycotts of 1980. Research by Scharf and Pinnock on non-student gangs in coloured areas of the Western Cape provides some insight into the involvement of gangs in political protest in this period. Gangs were more numerous and prominent in coloured areas in the Western Cape than elsewhere, and during the 1980 school boycotts they did become involved in action. The form of their involvement was very specific, however. According to Scharf, they were more interested in looting and stealing than participating in 'political' activity:

The school-children challenged the state to meet their demands by organised, restrained political action, whereas the gangs exploited the momentary inability of the police to cope with any contingencies in a glut of opportunistic materialism. When I questioned them about their role in the unrest, Joker and his entire gang gleefully responded that 'wanneer die studente politiek maak, dan doen gam free shopping' (when the students make politics, then we go shopping for free).

Such opportunities were relatively rare during this period. Scharf reports that the gangs were dismissive of politics: 'Some of them had internalised government propaganda that labelled all political dissent as communistic.' Gang and political consciousness only very rarely merged. The leader of the gang which Scharf concentrated his research on, Joker, was suspicious of and almost hostile to civic organisation. The gangs routinely competed for police favours; Joker met with the police weekly, exchanging information for protection and even money.[41]

The relationship between gangs and student activists in coloured areas in 1980 contrasts with accounts of Soweto in 1976 (by Mzamane, for example).

The major activities of youth organisations during the early 1980s were political recruitment and education rather than protest. Youth organisations and activists frequently engaged in social, charitable and civic activities in order to recruit new members, build good relations with older township residents, and chip away at a pervasive wariness of 'political' activity. Several youth groups undertook house-to-house work, canvassing township residents' views on civic and other issues, prior to taking up civic issues with the local authorities. Youth activists in Kagiso prepared for the formation of the local civic in 1981 with such house-to-house visits. Malayo members similarly canvassed residents' views.[42]

Many youth groups performed charitable work, whether through fundraising or more direct support. This was especially true in some Indian areas where there was widespread wariness of 'political' activity. The Helping Hands youth group in Chatsworth, and the Lenasia-based Time to Learn project were prominent examples of such community-oriented groups (both affiliated to the UDF in 1983).[43]

The Tumahole Students Organisation (TSO) provides a good example of the activities – and effects – of youth groups during this period. It was formed in June 1980, primarily through the efforts of a student who had just returned from Fort Hare University.

---

41 Scharf: 'The Impact of Liquor', pp. 114-5. See also Scharf: 'Street gangs, survival and political consciousness in the eighties', unpublished paper presented at the Roots and Realities Conference, University of Cape Town, July 1986.
42 Interviews: Kagiso 1989-1990 and Durban 1992.
43 Naidoo: 'The politics of youth resistance', and interview by Frederikse; interview with M Valli Moosa.

TSO drew a range of young people, including school students, into drama productions and contests. These were held for fundraising and social reasons, as well as conveying of political messages. Plays took up political themes, and were apparently well-received.

TSO secured the use of the community hall as an overnight shelter for pensioners waiting to collect their quarterly pensions. Members would also help with funeral preparations, including raising money for coffins; they would then raise political issues during the night vigil or funeral service. Funds were also raised to help pay the rent of impoverished families whose breadwinners had died, for school books and uniforms for poor students, for local churches, as well as for a kindergarten and a creche. The group itself held regular discussions on political topics, and celebrated days such as 16 June. Through these activities, TSO both raised political issues and earned the support and respect of other residents of the township.[44]

Summary

During the period between 1976 and 1984 the youth re-emerged as a central category in opposition politics. In the mid-1970s militant young people were generally described and seem to have thought of themselves as students, even if they had left school and not found work. During the 1976-77 uprisings the term 'youth' was used to describe unidentified young people who engaged in direct action without evidence of political motivation. In the aftermath of 1976-77 the category of youth was reconstructed. The students who had participated in and 'graduated' from the uprisings required an identity separate from students and sought organisations through which they could remain politically active. Both inside the country and in exile the term 'youth' was adopted in 1980-81 to refer to these highly politicised and purposeful ex-students.

Most youth organisations during 1979-83 engaged in community-oriented rather than overtly political activities, in order to avoid police harassment and build support. The youth congresses

---

44 TSO is discussed further in Seekings: 'Political Mobilisation in Tumahole'.

formed in 1983 adopted a more political profile, reflecting the changing times and the growing national political opposition to the state, especially its constitutional reforms. During this whole period youth organisations were by-and-large groups of young, and relatively well-educated, activists; unemployed youth rarely became involved, and gangs were generally opposed to youth activists. Many youth organisations earned considerable local support through their charitable and civic activities; they provided the personpower for wider political campaigns, and provided political education for many students and other young people.

Chapter Three

Youth and the township revolt, 1984-1988

Between 1984 and 1986 widespread protests over a variety of issues grew into an unprecedented revolt in South Africa's townships. From the middle of 1984 onwards, protests occurred around educational grievances, increased rents and service charges in townships, and the new tri-cameral parliament (which was not only racially-structured but excluded Africans). State repression and popular defiance escalated, each exacerbating the other.

In mid-1985 the state declared a partial State of Emergency covering most of the PWV and Eastern Cape; this was later extended to the Western Cape. Notwithstanding this, consumer and rent boycotts continued to proliferate, as did violent attacks on township councillors and many state-owned buildings. In mid-1986 a nationwide State of Emergency was imposed, and opposition activists were imprisoned *en masse*. Many protests continued, but the revolt was temporarily checked by the massive state clampdown.

Accounts of the mid-1980s routinely ascribe to the youth a central and leading role in this resistance. Sitas writes of South Africa being 'engulfed in a black youth uprising', while Hyslop wrote (in 1988):

> [T]here can be few parallels for the dominating role that young people have played in the political conflict in South Africa over the last decade ... Students and youth formed the shock troops of the outbreak, mounting pickets, organising mass actions and engaging in street battles with the army and the police ... [During 1984-85] youth became the foot soldiers of a battle for control of the township streets.

In similar vein, Webster wrote:

> The youth were consistently in the forefront of community struggles. Reports from around the country reveal that even in rural areas, communities which had been dormant were first galvanised by the youth. They emerged as the most militant resisters, the foot soldiers of the struggle.[1]

Notwithstanding this prominence in accounts of the period, the category of 'youth' and the activities of its members are rarely analysed. Bundy, in his important analysis, begins with the assumption that the youth made a 'distinctive contribution' to political struggle; he proceeds to explain why, but without spelling out what it was that youth actually *did*, and how this differed from the actions of other or older people.[2]

The composition of the youth in this period of township revolt is either avoided or inadequately dealt with in the existing literature. The youth of the mid-1980s were not the same as the youth of 1979-84. In both periods the youth were generally understood (within opposition politics) to refer to people who appeared to be politicised and involved in activity apparently focused on explicitly political objectives.

The category of youth was reconstructed as the scope of political activity itself broadened, with protest, confrontation and violence becoming more and more widespread, and liberation seeming imminent. Youth organisations proliferated, and the num-

---

[1] Sitas: 'The Comrades Movement', p. 631; Hyslop: 'School student movements', pp. 183, 193; Webster, D: 'Repression and the State of Emergency', *South African Review* 4 (Johannesburg: Ravan, 1987), p. 154.

[2] Bundy: 'Street sociology', p. 303.

ber of people involved in them grew rapidly. Many others came to be seen as youth through their participation in direct action or other forms of 'political' struggle. The changing composition and character of the youth was thus the product – and in turn a cause – of the changing political context.

National youth organisation

Large numbers of young people were drawn into protest and conflict, and thereby into the category of youth, during the township revolt. ANC-aligned youth organisations were formed in townships and rural areas across the country. The scale and importance of youth mobilisation and organisation gave new impetus to moves to form an ANC-aligned national youth organisation. But progress remained slow. Proposed campaigns around International Youth Year failed to provide the hoped for focus for national organisation building. It was only in March 1987 that the South African Youth Congress (Sayco) was formally launched. Less than one year later, in February 1988, Sayco was restricted, and soon after its entire leadership was detained under the nationwide State of Emergency.

Some national co-ordination was provided through interim youth structures and the UDF during 1985-87. At a conference held in Durban during January 1985, a committee was elected to prepare the formation of a national youth organisation. June 1985 was optimistically proposed as the launch date. A second committee, convened by Dan Montsisi, was elected to co-ordinate a campaign around International Youth Year. The campaign would, it was hoped, provide a focus for national youth organisation comparable to the focus which the constitutional reforms had provided for the UDF during 1983-84.[3]

Neither of these committees made much progress during 1985. June went by without even the prospect of an imminent launch of a national youth organisation, and the International Youth Year campaign failed to get off the ground. There were several reasons for this:

---

3   Interviews: Nkomfe, Ntombela.

☆ organisations struggled to keep up with the rapidly changing political situation;
☆ state repression inhibited organisational development, with large numbers of youth activists detained under the partial State of Emergency after July 1985, while others were pulled into UDF structures to take the places of its detained or jailed leaders; and
☆ youth organisations were weakened by debilitating ideological and factional disputes.

The building of national organisation lagged behind, but local level youth organisations were carried along by mass mobilisation and defiance. During 1985-86 unprecedented numbers of people, many of them young, were drawn into protest against the state, and youth organisations proliferated in townships and rural areas across the country. The insurrectionary beliefs of many youth leaders led them to prioritise struggle rather than organisation-building. Some believed that organisation would be developed through struggle, but in practice the efforts put into consumer and rent boycotts, together with more violent forms of direct action, meant that the development of a national youth organisation was neglected.

Many prominent youth leaders were called upon to direct their organisational efforts into the UDF rather than youth structures. As a result, many became involved in UDF regional structures, especially in 1985 when much of the UDF's initial leadership was on trial. Youth leaders on the Transvaal regional executive committee, for example, included Paul Mashatile (Alexandra), Eddie Makue, Murphy Morobe and Dan Montsisi (all from Soweto), and Matthews Sathekge and Titus Mafolo (from Pretoria). In mid-1985, when many of this second generation of UDF leaders were detained, it was a third wave of youth activists who stepped in as interim officials.

Detentions under the partial State of Emergency and the Internal Security Act also accounted for many youth activists. The Detainees Parents Support Committee estimated that sixty per cent of detainees in the first three months of the State of Emergency were aged under twenty-five. A total of eight thousand people were detained during the first Emergency (July 1985 to March 1986). An estimated twenty-two thousand had been arrested and charged with various offences, including public violence.[4] Detailed statistics on the composition of these totals is not readily available, but it is clear that young people figured very prominently, while large numbers of identifiable leaders were either detained or forced into hiding. This retarded progress towards a national organisation.

Ideological disputes further inhibited moves towards regional and national organisation. The most widespread dispute involved factions based around 'Freeway House' and the acting UDF leadership respectively. The 'Freeway House' group (named after the building in Johannesburg which housed several service organisations with extensive resources) came to adopt a left critique of the UDF leadership, and were labelled as 'ultra-leftists' by their rivals. It is unclear, however, to what extent the ideological character of the conflict was its cause, or developed subsequent to division. However, the dispute became very bitter.[5]

The dispute was particularly intense in Natal, with two groups of youth activists based around a joint NYO/IYY committee on the one hand, and the Diakonia-based Youth Forum on the other. Progress towards a Natal youth organisation was paralysed until May 1986 when a joint meeting was held to establish an interim Natal Youth Congress. The NYO/IYY leadership swept the elections, although it was alleged that they had brought bogus youth organisations to vote for them. The Youth Forum group were thereafter marginalised.[6]

As a result of these various factors, the proposed NYO was not formed, and the campaign around International Youth Year floundered. Even early in the year it was the 'parent' UDF which provided most of the impetus for action around the IYY. Late in 1985 the IYY national co-ordinator reported that activities had been completely disrupted by emergency regulations; the national co-ordinating committee had not met in over six months (since March, four months prior to the State of Emergency!), and the

---

4   Coleman, M and Webster, D: 'Repression and Detention in South Africa', *South African Review* 3 (Johannesburg: Ravan, 1986).
5   See for example the UDF-IYY National Co-ordinating Committee's 'Brief Report to the Regions', signed D Montsisi, undated, October/November 1985.
6   Interviews: Dlamini, Tsenoli, Naidoo.

national co-ordinator himself was in hiding.[7] Another date which had been proposed for the NYO launch passed in April 1986 with little sign of progress.

Paradoxically it was under the even more repressive conditions of the second, national State of Emergency (from June 1986) that national youth organisation finally began to cohere. In July 1986 a national interim co-ordinating committee was elected at an underground consultative conference in Cape Town. Peter Mokaba was elected interim national education officer with a brief to solve the ideological divisions which still persisted. In late October 1986 a further workshop was held at Broederstroom, outside Pretoria, to debate and draft key documents and prepare for a national launch.[8]

Sayco was finally launched, clandestinely, at the University of the Western Cape in late March 1987. It claimed 1 200 local affiliates, a signed-up membership of over half-a-million, and a support base of two million. It thus claimed to be the biggest youth grouping of its kind in South African history.

Sayco adopted an unambiguously political stance. This was reflected in its leadership – the president, Peter Mokaba, was a former Robben Islander – and its chosen symbols: the slogan of 'Freedom or Death: Victory is Certain', the combined colours of the ANC and Cosatu, and the logo of a fist holding a black flag. Sayco had a federal structure, comprising ten regional youth congresses to which local youth congresses affiliated. Its federal structure was in large part due to the need to accommodate the different points of view (or factions) which had delayed the formation for so long.[9]

The formation of Sayco was followed by the formation of regional ANC-aligned youth structures, while the exiled ANC itself upgraded its youth structures outside the country. Like Sayco itself, most of the regional structures (and many local structures) had to be launched in secret under the repressive conditions of the State of Emergency. The Free State Youth Congress was even launched outside the region, in Durban. The Northern Transvaal

---

7 See IYY: 'Brief Report'.
8 Interviews: Ntombela, Mokaba.
9 Niddrie, D: 'New National Youth Congress Launched', *Work In Progress* 47 (April 1987); *New Nation*, 12 April 1990.

Youth Congress was the largest regional structure, claiming 225 affiliates with a total membership of 120 000 youth. The Eastern Cape region claimed 110 000 members. In August the ANC held its second 'National' Youth Conference in exile, in Tanzania (like the previous conference of 1982). The ANC formed a National Youth Committee headed by ex-Saso leader Jackie Selebi.[10]

Sayco embarked on a series of national campaigns, although these were constrained by the State of Emergency. One of Sayco's first campaigns focused on youths on death row. Initially called the 'Save the 32' campaign, it had to be renamed 'Save the Patriots' when the number of death row prisoners rose. Sayco's other campaigns included actions to isolate the police (especially the notorious *kitskonstabels*), popularise the Freedom Charter, organise the unemployed, and so on.[11]

Sayco and its regional structures forged high profile alliances with those trade unions affiliated (after its December 1985 launch) to the Congress of South African Trade Unions (Cosatu). Cosatu was relatively free to organise during 1986-88, and undertook some of the activities previously performed by the UDF. In addition, the involvement of many unemployed youth in youth organisations created Sayco as an important ally for trade unions concerned about scab labour during strikes. Cosatu itself attempted to organise unemployed people into a trade union of the unemployed, but its National Unemployed Workers Co-ordinating Committee floundered. Sayco subscribed to the view of the ANC and UDF that the youth comprised a 'social group' rather than a class; it was the working class which was the backbone of the liberation struggle. The youth therefore had to work with workers' organisations.

In February 1988 Sayco, with a range of other organisations (including the Soweto and Cape Youth Congresses), was severely restricted by the state. Later in the year the Port Elizabeth Youth Congress was also restricted. At the time, Sayco claimed more than one million members. Sayco's entire leadership was detained

---

10 *City Press*, 2 August 1987; *The Star,* 1 July 1987; *Grassroots*, May 1987; *Sechaba* (November 1987).
11 'Learning to live in the shadows', *Work in Progress* 53 (April/May 1988).

in August, and many of the leaders of its major local affiliates who had hitherto evaded the police were finally detained.

This section has focused on ANC-aligned or Charterist youth organisations, but there were of course other youth organisations aligned with other political traditions or movements. Non-Charterist youth organisations included the Inkatha Youth Brigade (with a claimed membership of just over half-a-million in 1987), the Inyandza Youth Movement (in KaNgwane), and the Black Consciousness-aligned Azasm and Azanyu (the membership of which remains unclear).

Youth politics at local level

It was during the bitter conflict of the mid-1980s that the youth came to be seen as the driving force of township militancy. Their role in transforming the dream of liberation into an apparently imminent event led to their being celebrated as the 'young lions'; the association with the rising use of violent direct action led to their being denigrated as mal-socialised savages. In reality, the so-called youth in the mid-1980s included politically astute strategists as well as violent individualists, and many other young people besides. The category of youth was an amalgam of many different types of young people, with a wide range of goals and motivations.

Youth organisations were formed in townships and rural areas across the country, and their claimed membership grew rapidly. In late 1983 there were less than fifty youth organisations affiliated to the UDF (excluding the church-based groups in the Western Cape). Few of these had a membership, in the sense of people regularly attending meetings, much higher than a hundred. Their total membership was thus probably less than ten thousand. By mid-1987, Sayco's regional structures were claiming 1 200 local affiliates, with a signed-up membership of over half-a-million, and a support base of two million (although Sayco claimed just one million members a year later). Even taking account of considerable exaggeration, there was clearly a massive growth in terms of both organisations and membership.

The relationship between formal youth organisation and the 'youth' also changed during this period. While the rapid growth of youth organisation both reflected and contributed to the growing insurrection, patterns of informal organisation became as important as formal youth organisation. Indeed, leading progressive activists were often concerned that youth militancy should be provided with direction lest it turned against society rather than just the state – as, sometimes, it did. Lodge goes so far as to suggest that 'notwithstanding its martial rhetoric, Sayco's main function was to bring the youth into line, and to check any propensity to challenge the authority of adults'.[12] Sayco was certainly concerned to provide the 'correct' political direction, but this was more a case of harnessing and sustaining the militancy of the youth than limiting it. The concern to provide direction was often subordinated to the objective of escalating resistance.

Many youth leaders believed that the apartheid state was on the verge of collapse, and that any and all forms of pressure should be exerted on it. As Straker writes:

From the perspective of the youth, this was a time of euphoria as well as terror. They had a newfound sense of power and a vision of the future. They saw themselves as leading the older generation to freedom. Liberation was believed to be in sight and they were to be the authors of it.[13]

Bundy writes of the 'triumphalism' of the youth.[14] The ANC was calling for people's war, encouraging militancy among its 'footsoldiers'. There was little concern with how opposition was organised, who was involved, or why. This causes problems for researchers trying to identify, after the event, who the 'youth' were. Many of the youth were unknown to each other, and even leaders of the formal youth (or student) organisations were often ignorant as to the identity, let alone motivations, of many of the people prominently involved in acts of resistance.

---

12 Lodge, T and Nasson, B: *All, Here and Now: Black Politics in South Africa in the 1980s*, (Cape Town: David Philip, 1992), p. 103.
13 Straker: *Faces in the Revolution*, p. 19.
14 Bundy: 'Street Sociology'.

From trial records and interviews we can begin to sketch a picture of the youth – or rather, pictures of the youth, since the most striking feature of this group was its heterogeneity and fluidity. The following section draws especially on accounts of the youth in two townships: Duduza, on the East Rand, and Leandra, in the Eastern Transvaal. The material on Duduza is drawn from trials and subsequent interviews.[15] The material on Leandra's youth is drawn from Straker's study, *Faces in the Revolution*.

The leadership of formal youth organisation

Let us first consider the leadership of formal youth organisations, ie primarily youth congresses but also Cosas branches which in some areas played a leading role among the youth at a local level during 1984-85. For the most part, this leadership comprised politically articulate activists, motivated by political idealism and a sense of participation in political change. Even when youth organisations were formed amidst violent conflict, eloquence, intellectual sophistication and organisational enthusiasm were widely regarded as qualifications for formal leadership. Many leaders came from better-off households.[16] Brewer refers to these activists as 'educated labour'.[17]

Many youth activists were students or former students who had come through Cosas or semi-political youth clubs where they were influenced by older political activists. Others were politicised at home by older family members. University students often helped organise in their home townships during vacations. For example, students from university or colleges in Cape Town and Oudtshoorn

---

15   *State vs Montoedi and 11 others; State vs Mazibuko and 6 others; State vs Motaung and 10 others.*
16   See the description of the 'typical' student leader in 'Youth is at the core of the unrest in townships' in *The Star*, 5 August 1985.
17   Brewer, J: 'Black protest in South Africa's crisis: a comment on Legassick', *African Affairs* 85, p. 339 (April 1986). Brewer wrote this before less schooled individuals were clearly drawn into the membership and (informal) leadership of the youth.

played a key role in forming the Zanokhanyo Youth Organisation in Beaufort West.[18] Swilling reports that the key characteristic of the Uitenhage Youth Congress leadership was that they were relatively well-educated:

> [T]his group had a remarkably clear political ideology derived from a reading of the alternative media, banned literature (usually ANC material) and some well used Marxist texts (especially Lenin) published by Progress and Lawrence and Wishart ...[19]

The Uitenhage youth leaders were mostly in their mid-twenties, and included students, workers, and unemployed people. Young workers, together with university and school students, generally predominated in the formal leadership of youth organisation, but there were also many young unemployed people. This reflected several factors. Firstly, not all politicised school students found employment after leaving school. Some ex-student activists also chose to remain unemployed – or at least did not seek work too eagerly – in order to have time to organise. Secondly, significant numbers of young politicised workers were dismissed by employers (sometimes following strike action). While unemployed, many put their energies into political (ie 'youth' organisation. For example, two leading members of the Tumahole Youth Congress were former shop stewards in the Chemical Workers Industrial Union (CWIU) who had been laid off from Sasol in Secunda. Former CWIU shop stewards from Sasol played a similarly central role in organising the youth in other Orange Free State townships.[20]

The initial youth leadership in Duduza comprised older school students, almost all male teenagers, from both petty bourgeois and working class backgrounds. Several had previously been involved in a short-lived youth club, and a number had held a placard demonstration against community council elections in late 1983. But

---

18 Interview: T Mlonyeni.
19 Swilling, M: '"Because your yard is too big": squatters, the local state, and dual power in Uitenhage, 1985-1986', paper presented at the African Studies Institute seminar, University of the Witwatersrand, March 1988, p. 3.
20 Interviews: S Magashule, P Legoale.

they were initially cut off from, and even ignorant of, national student politics. The student leaders were among the better educated young township residents, the 'successes' rather than the 'failures' of the school system. In late 1984 they formed a Cosas branch, and in early 1985 a youth congress.

The core membership of youth organisations – those members who regularly attended meetings and participated in formal organisational activity – was generally limited in numbers and composition. In most cases the core membership probably included up to fifty activists, mostly high school or college students, or school and college graduates.[21] In some townships (such as Alexandra) this core membership might have been larger, but it was rarely higher than one hundred.

Confrontation and informal youth leaders

The increasingly violent character of township politics in the mid-1980s transformed the nature of leadership and, in so doing, a second set of youth leaders emerged. This leadership – and the supporting organisation – was informal. It comprised young men whose skills lay in strategising or executing direct action, including violence, rather than in intellectual debate. They organised and led defence against attacks, as well as 'pre-emptive' attacks against known opponents.

The formal and informal youth leadership often overlapped. 'Ricky' from Leandra, for example, was aged fifteen in 1985, and had been on the executive of the local youth congress. Amidst rising violence, Ricky (a regular church-goer) formed his own group of experienced 'destroyers'. Straker's description of Ricky suggests he was a thoughtful leader and strategist, motivated by clear political ideals. But he believed that liberation required direct action:

---

21 This was the case in, for example, Beaufort West and Tumahole.

Youth and the township revolt, 1984-88

> *In reflecting on this period, he recalls these times as heady ones. There was a sense of euphoria in the township, especially among the youth ... a sense that the initiative was theirs.*[22]

Action, including violent action, provided a sense of collective power after years of subordination under apartheid. Ricky endorsed violence only within the context of legitimate and just armed resistance. He was opposed to 'gratuitous' violence, and to actions informed by personal motives of revenge or gain rather than by widely accepted values.

In Duduza, the student/Cosas activists became involved in organising direct, and later violent, action. Their political idealism combined with conditions in the country as a whole to encourage some of them to escalate resistance. In interviews, student leaders of the time recall that their aim was to make Duduza ungovernable: 'It was a national thing; liberation was imminent; we just wanted power ... We thought the youth could liberate South Africa.' They thought of themselves as part of the national liberation struggle, and prioritised playing a role in it. The absence of formal organisation among the students encouraged direct action, lest students in Duduza fell behind their peers elsewhere.

But other youth leaders had not been previously involved in formal leadership. Of ten prominent young Duduza people charged with treason,[23] four were involved in formal organisation: one in the civic association, one in Cosas, and two more in the Duduza Youth Congress. The other six were prominent in informal groups. This indicates the extent to which leading roles in the youth were assumed by people outside of formal youth or other organisational structures. Of the ten, one was a self-employed carpenter, one a matric student, four were workers, three were unemployed, and the tenth described himself as a 'freelance artist'. At least two of the accused were prominent gang members. One (the 'artist') was known as 'America' because he liked the good life. He was said not to be politically informed, but was a leader because he was strong and intelligent; and was said to be widely feared. Another was a heavy drinker, and was apparently regarded as a criminal.

---

22 Straker: *Faces in the Revolution*, p. 24.
23 *State vs Montoedi and others*.

Violent conflict became most extreme in Natal. Kentridge writes that the leadership was 'often split between those with an aptitude for political and military strategy, and those with an aptitude for fighting.'[24]

The youth in general

The general membership as well as leadership of the youth broadened during the township uprisings. The composition of the youth varied between areas, and over time. In most areas, however, the first youth to become politically prominent were student activists, and the bulk of the youth in initial incidents of confrontation were protesting students. When conflict extended out of the schoolyard and onto the street, and protest escalated into violence, non-students became involved.

The changing composition of the youth was reflected in unrest fatalities. Of the sixteen people killed before November 1984 in the PWV region, at least ten and possibly twelve were students. From early November (when a massive regional stayaway was held in the PWV, accompanied by widespread violent conflict), a rising proportion of fatalities were older people or non-students. As we shall see below, the involvement of non-student youth initially led to tensions in some townships, where students accused 'undisciplined' non-students of 'hijacking' protests, and parents accused them of generally rowdy behaviour.

In some areas, students seem to have predominated in each stage of conflict. In coloured areas of the Western Cape, students constituted a very high proportion of the youth, even during the period of street conflict following the school-based protests. These are the youth whom Bundy considers in his widely-cited article.[25]

---

24 Kentridge, M: *An Unofficial War: Inside the Conflict in Pietermaritzburg* (Cape Town: David Philip, 1990), p. 53.
25 Bundy: 'Street sociology'. Bundy ignores forms of youth struggle which involved non-students, or did not involve students as students — for example, in the enforcement of consumer boycotts. Compare with Cole, J: *Crossroads: the politics of reform and repression, 1976-1986* (Johannesburg: Ravan, 1987).

They were unusually educated and articulate, the products of the relatively open political debate that characterised the area.

The involvement of students in protests generally reflected a convergence of educational and civic grievances, and national political concerns. Not only did conditions in schools provide a strong impetus to protest, but many students were highly politicised and concerned about civic issues.

Students were not only motivated by educational grievances, civic concerns or political idealism. A sense of adventure, even of fun, encouraged many of them to participate. Straker writes that Ricky, who was in many ways a political idealist,

> *described with obvious pride a number of episodes in which the group had attacked various buildings and houses. It was clear that he related to each event as an adventure, that there was a game-like quality in the enterprise. In fact, as he told me about each episode, he became quite childlike in his enthusiasm and animation.*[26]

For many youth the sense of adventure or fun was paramount. To repeat Mzamane's comment on 1976, it was (among other things) 'a glorious game'. One of Straker's interviewees, 'Sisi', told her that many or even most participants were just swept up in events. According to Sisi,

> *They joined for their enjoyment – not really out of real understanding of the issues and certainly not to work. They were attracted by the slogans and the songs. They enjoyed the toyi-toyi and the singing and throwing stones and the running away from the police. They liked action and were not really keen on spending hours in meetings listening to the problems of the community and strategising how best to approach them.*[27]

'Pretty' was another member of the Leandra youth, whom Straker describes as a conformist. Pretty joined a group of students who raised complaints about conditions in school. She supported the complaints, but was more attracted by the protesters' vitality:

---

26 Straker: *Faces in the Revolution*, p. 25.
27 'Sisi', quoted by Straker: *Faces in the Revolution*, pp. 30-31.

I enjoyed the freedom songs, and the toyi-toyi; they made me feel happy. I joined in when they sang and after that they would usually tell me when they had meetings and I would attend. At that time I did not really understand much about what was happening. I gleaned some information from the meetings. But all the people I spoke to were not well informed, like me.[28]

Straker suggests that Pretty's participation in the struggle was not motivated by a critical understanding of the issues or by socio-political idealism. Rather, she sought to conform to the group. The situation was similar in Duduza. Even among the students, as one student leader arrogantly put it, there were few people with any 'political education': 'most youth were just doing it for fun', and withdrew from 'political' activity when repression mounted under the State of Emergency'.[29]

This view, and Straker's profiles, point to the importance of the development of a culture of militaristic camaraderie. At one level this was a culture of the toyi-toyi and of freedom songs. At another, it was based on social and political collective action rooted in the Freedom Charter's political ideology, the confrontational messages of Radio Freedom and the reality of street violence.[30] It was an extremely attractive culture. As Lodge writes: 'For growing numbers of children, the militarized subculture inspired by Umkhonto heroics had a more compelling attraction than the routine of even the most liberated classrooms.' And as a twenty year-old from Cradock commented: 'We are getting another education – a political education which is more important now.'[31]

Another attraction of participation in collective action was the affirmation that it provided. Straker refers to another of the Leandra youth, 'Isaac', as a 'hero in search of a script'. Isaac, who was only thirteen years old in 1985, participated as a way of giving meaning and direction to his life. Straker describes Isaac as trying

---

28 Straker: *Faces in the Revolution*, p. 55.
29 Interviews: student leaders (Duduza).
30 Sitas suggests a number of further components of the distinctive culture of the comrades which developed in Natal – see 'The Comrades', pp. 6-7.
31 Lodge and Nasson: *All, Here and Now, p. 102;* 'The kids who don't care', *The Star*, 13 October 1985.

to play the romantic role of a warrior-hero, blurring macho fantasies and reality. The role combined socio-political ideals with an emphasis on personal action and courage. Beneath the tough image, however, Isaac remained caring and vulnerable, and he had strong misgivings after several incidents of violence.

Isaac sought to be a hero, understanding this in terms of sociopolitical ideals. Other youth sought affirmation in different ways, by doing whatever their contemporaries were doing, but more so. When the group was angry, these youth would selflessly take risks. Straker writes that 'this may be of benefit to the community and will bring the individual the affirmation and approval that is sought'; at the same time, however, 'their drive for affirmation' could also drive them 'over the edge into socially disruptive behaviour in order to meet their exhibitionist needs'. Straker categorises these youth as 'conduits', who are

> *responsive to the collective mood and act in conformity with it. They are ... reactive rather than proactive ... Just as the conduits give expression to the moods of the group, so they too use it as a vehicle for the discharge of their own emotions. They lack a clearly defined sense of self and use the group in their search for definition.*[32]

Straker's profiles show how conditions were created in which people with only a weak sense of the political issues involved would participate for the adventure or the affirmation. Their participation itself could serve to raise levels of action, and even of violence.

Participation in violence

Rising levels of conflict encouraged people to behave in unusual ways. Normally non-violent people acted violently, for a variety of reasons. Increasing conflict also provided opportunities for, and attracted, chronically violent people. Several people who were widely understood to be criminal or anti-social at heart were among the Duduza youth discussed above. Straker provides a pro-

---

32   Straker: *Faces in the Revolution*, p. 46.

file of 'Silas', one such young man from Leandra, who became a highly valued comrade in 1985-86 because of his physical strength and bravery. But Silas's association with violence predated political conflict: 'He reports that for as long as he can remember he has had difficulty restraining his temper and his inclination to physical violence.' His more serious actions included attacking someone with an axe and stabbing people in fights.[33]

There were probably many people like Silas. Participation in 'political' struggle provided an opportunity for them to harness their machismo and aggression for a reputable cause, and earn respect from others, both as fighters and as heroes. As Cross says:

> Gangsters can do things like throw petrol bombs and hijack cars that normal people must be first taught to do, so there was a real space for the expression of gang culture in the struggle.[34]

Kentridge elaborates on this with respect to *comtsotsis* in Natal:

> The comtsotsis assaulted and robbed people and shops; they preyed on commuters and mugged workers on pay-day, much like tsotsis (gangsters) in other parts of the country. The difference was that they explained that their actions were part of a political strategy.

He quotes a pro-ANC civic leader on these *tsotsis*:

> Some of them were always tsotsis. They fought in gangs before the war started, but they were quite small. Then later some went to Inkatha, some came to us. They said that Inkatha was very bad and violent and they wanted to help the community. And they are good fighters when the violence starts, but when you are only a fighter a war is good business. You can commit crimes and pretend you are still fighting the war. Some of them are genuinely believing in the UDF, but they get — how should I put this? — a taste for fighting. They can satisfy this appetite when violence escalates, but when it diminishes they have fewer targets and they get restless.[35]

---

33 Straker: *Faces in the Revolution*, pp. 73-8.
34 Cross, quoted in *Weekly Mail*, 8 February 1990.
35 Kentridge: *An Unofficial War*, p. 67.

Machismo and aggression were not restricted to gang members alone. Nor were they simply the result of general social, economic or political discontent. Campbell has argued, with respect to violence in Natal, that high levels of violence are related to what she terms a 'crisis of masculinity'. Violence, she suggests, is a compensatory mechanism for men whose masculinity has been undermined by their powerlessness in other respects, such as economic powerlessness resulting from unemployment. Membership of the 'comrades' provided an opportunity for the reassertion of male power.[36] To many, including unemployed people and those with a history of violence, participation in violent 'political' struggle provided a means of building self-esteem and earning social acclamation.

This might suggest a link between unemployment and involvement in violence. Indeed, many accounts suggest that the youth during 1985-86 comprised primarily the 'unemployed', and apparently have such a link in mind. Several authors incorrectly suggest that youth congresses comprised mostly unemployed people during 1983-84. Bundy writes of youth congresses having 'their base in the urban unemployed'.[37]

Swilling writes that the Port Elizabeth and Uitenhage Youth Congresses were 'formed by small groups of unemployed youths', and most of the youth in these areas were 'the largely uneducated unemployed' or 'lumpenproletariat'. He identifies two types among the unemployed. Some, he suggests, were people with a background in student politics who had become disillusioned with non-violent tactics, for whom violence or direct action was a strategic choice. Other youth were former petty criminals who participated in political struggle 'largely because by adopting an anti-state resistance ideology [they] could legitimise [their] illegal activities ...' Swilling also writes of 'the politicisation of the unemployed youth', who were 'badly educated', mostly from squatter areas. They 'were drawn into political activity without substantially altering their position on the fringes of legality.'[38]

---

36 Campbell, C: 'Learning to kill? Masculinity, the family and violence in Natal', *Journal of Southern African Studies* 18/3 (September 1992).
37 Bundy: 'Street sociology', p. 317. See also Hyslop: 'School student movements', p. 193.
38 Swilling: 'Because your yard is so big'; and Swilling: 'Stayaways,

References to the 'unemployed' imply that the people concerned were

- available for direct action (because they were not at work or school, for example);
- somehow 'desperate' (being poor, ill-educated, ill-housed, and without opportunity);
- without responsibilities, and therefore irresponsible or reckless.

All three of these assumptions are questionable. It is unclear whether there is any unambiguous qualitative difference between the unemployed and the employed/student population in each respect. In addition, it is unclear how significant these factors should be in an explanation of why certain people participated in direct action.

Many young people on township streets from 1984 were 'unemployed' in the narrow sense of not being employed. And, in the Eastern Cape, it may have been the case that these particular types of 'unemployed' youth were in the majority. But the youth also included many other types of 'unemployed' people. Many were students boycotting school, or forced out when schools were closed down, but whose outlook remained that of students. Furthermore, as Straker's profiles indicate, there were diverse reasons for participating in direct action.

More importantly, evidence from townships such as Duduza indicates that a range of employed and unemployed people, as well as students, participated in the kinds of action generally attributed to the youth. In the evenings, on weekends and during stayaways, many working people and students joined crowds. Straker was told by one of the Leandra youth that 'most' local people took part in incidents such as an attack on a local white-owned store. As Straker puts it: 'There was a sense of shared purpose, a feeling in the crowd that at last they were standing up for their rights and being effective.'[39]

Sitas makes a similar point about the composition of the 'comrades' in Durban:

---

urban protest and the state' in *South African Review* 3, pp. 35-6.
39 Straker: *Faces in the Revolution*, p. 24.

Youth and the township revolt, 1984-88

It is not helpful crudely to identify or equate 'comrades' with black youth unemployment. Yes, most comrades are young (below 35); yes, most comrades come from embattled working class homesteads and households; yes, most of their cultural codes emerge outside households and kinship relations; yes, many are unemployed. But among the phenomenon called comrades we will find full wage-earners, informal sector vendors, university graduates, political activists, schoolchildren, shop-stewards, petty criminals and lumpenproletarians.[40]

The profiles of the sixty-odd youth in Straker's study do not reveal the composition of the youth in general, even in Leandra. They were all, in one way or another, conspicuously involved in action in Leandra, which is why they had to leave the township. Their prominence suggests that they were regular, rather than occasional, participants in action. In other words, they constituted the core of the youth. To identify the constitution of the mass of youth who were occasionally involved, we need to examine particular, atypical incidents.

One such incident involved the murder of an alleged informer, Maki Skhosana, at a funeral in Duduza in July 1985 – a killing recorded by foreign television and broadcast crews as a grisly backdrop to the declaration of the first State of Emergency. Eleven people were charged in court with participating in the killing.[41] None of them exhibited any clear 'political' consciousness; most (it seems) had not previously attended political meetings. Nine of the eleven were neither students nor had they been students in the recent past. In contrast to Duduza's student leaders, the eleven were unambiguously working class: they were not well educated, came from poor families, and were either unemployed or in poorly paying jobs. Their ages ranged (at the time of the killing) from fourteen to thirty-one, with five aged twenty-five or over and only two under twenty-one.

Few corresponded, however, to the stereotypical *tsotsi* youth without any responsibilities. Five of the eleven were female. 'Rebecca' lived in a shack with her four-year old child and its father, a local worker. 'Lulama' had left school during Standard Five

---

40 Sitas: 'The Comrades', p. 6.
41 *State vs Motaung and others*.

because she was pregnant, and since then had worked on and off as a tea-maker in local offices. Of the men, 'Jabu' had left school during Standard Four, and worked as a labourer until being retrenched in February 1985. 'Fuzile' had left school during Standard Five, and was a machine operator. 'Aubrey' had left school during Standard Four because his brother, who had paid his fees, died. He worked at an old-age home. Several were regular church-goers. The attack on Skhosana was initiated, it seems, by a seventeen-year old student, who had previous convictions for house-breaking and assault.

This was, in sociological terms, a very mixed group of assailants. Why did these people participate in a brutal killing? Skhosana was killed at the funeral of four victims of police action. After the event, her killers said that Skhosana was widely blamed for the death of the four. But her killers had no individually specific motives for participating in the attack. Several had vague links with the four deceased — one of the killers had worked with one of the deceased; another was a friend of one of the deceaseds' mothers; but these links cannot explain their behaviour.

The participation of parents, students and workers as well as the unemployed or archetypical 'riff-raff' cannot be explained in terms of individual motivations abstracted from the immediate political context. It was not just fun, although a few people might have thought so. Nor was it propelled by national political consciousness. Rather, the killing resulted from a local political consciousness shaped by events in Duduza over the previous six or so months.

Skhosana's death was the culmination of several months of escalating violence between the community and the police, together with residents seen as allies of the 'system'. Local political consciousness was based less on the Freedom Charter than on councillors who abused power, policemen who shot at innocent residents with neither provocation nor need, and murderous vigilantes. Twenty residents died in four months of violence. Local dynamics thus defined 'us' and 'them', and made many people available for political action as part of the 'community' against the 'enemy'. Skhosana died because she was, possibly mistakenly, seen to be one of the enemy. However local political consciousness was not independent of national developments, with the perceived prospect of liberation, for example, helping to make militancy into a virtue.

In Duduza, as elsewhere, state repression played a crucial role in political polarisation and the intensification of confrontation. In the ten months before mid-1985, the security forces accounted for sixty per cent of all fatalities in overt political violence in South Africa,[42] and a similar proportion of the fatalities in Duduza itself. Not only did the police quickly resort to deadly force in both political and non-political situations, but many were involved (whether officially or not) in covert and illegal actions in Duduza as in many other townships. In Duduza there is considerable evidence to suggest that police were responsible for the night-time petrol-bombing of activists' houses, during which two girls were killed.

In successive court cases the state's own witnesses testified that they feared the police, and held them culpable for the petrol-bombing of activists' homes. The state's witnesses testified that this provoked them into revenge attacks on the police. One such witness, referred to as 'X4' because he gave his evidence in camera, admitted that he had participated in attacks on police houses. Under cross-examination X4, aged twenty-two and with a record of involvement in public violence, described his attitude to the police in the following way:

> *Q: What did you have against the police?*
> *X4: Well, it was because it was known at that stage that they were responsible to burn Mr Thobela's house.*
> *Q: When did that become known?*
> *X4: ... [B]efore the funeral, it was rumoured in the whole location.*
> *Q: Did you believe that [the police were responsible]?*
> *X4: Yes, I did believe that.*
> *Q: Did you believe that the police were capable of that?*
> *X4: Yes, I was believing that.*
> *Q: [Why would the police do that?]*

---

42 Figures from *Political Conflict in South Africa: Data Trends 1984-1988* (Durban, Indicator Project South Africa, 1988), p. 116.

X4: The only reason that I can think of is that it is because Thobela was also active in this struggle and the unrest.[43]

Fear of the police was pervasive. In another trial, every one of the state witnesses from Duduza (except police themselves) testified that they feared the police: 'I am very much afraid of the police', said one, whilst a fifteen year old said he was 'frightened of policemen'. A third agreed that he was 'very afraid' of the police, and the fourth testified that he had been assaulted by the police with sjamboks and batons at a funeral.[44]

Polarisation between police (and vigilantes) and the 'community' combined with police violence to provide the context within which a wide range of township residents themselves participated in violence. This was the local context in which leading Cosas members in Duduza procured hand grenades to use against local police and collaborators who they believed were responsible for petrol-bombing them. Four students from Duduza – and others from neighbouring townships – were killed when the grenades exploded in their hands. It was also the context in which, at a funeral of victims of police shooting, a range of people – including workers, women, parents and students – were drawn into the killing of Skhosana.[45]

Young children were among the widening range of participants in conflict. Pointing to the detention of children provided good propaganda material against the South African state, which defended itself by correctly pointing to the involvement of young children in acts of violence.[46] Just as the category of youth usually escaped definition, so the age-limit on children was rarely speci-

---

43 Evidence of X4, *State vs Montoedi and others*, p. 1, 158.
44 *State vs Motaung and others*, evidence of Miya, p. 157; Jele, p. 446; Tshabalala, p. 175; Mgubezelo, p. 119.
45 Moss, G: 'Duduza's Civil War', *Work in Progress* 47 (April 1987); for comparable accounts of other townships see Carter, C.: 'Community and Conflict: the Alexandra rebellion of 1986', *Journal of Southern African Studies* 18/1 (March 1992); Seekings, J: 'From Quiescence to People's Power: township politics in Kagiso, 1985-86', *Social Dynamics* 18/1 (June 1992).
46 See Seekings, J: 'A town where 14-year olds battle police' in *Weekly Mail*, 25 April 1986.

fied. But it was certainly the case that very young people – aged fifteen or younger – played an increasingly visible role in township conflict.

In Tumahole, for example, primary school students began to participate in limited acts of violence in 1986, although older people continued to play the major role in both protests and violence. The involvement of primary school children reflected many of the factors considered above: the attractive culture of militancy, the politicisation of consciousness through confrontation, the disruption and breakdown of schooling, and so on.[47]

Numbers of police informers were also among the many youth drawn in during this period. In Soweto, for example, there were so many suspected informers in one area that the local youth congress came to be known as the 'Protea Youth Congress' after the local Protea police station!

This section has suggested that both the composition and the motivations of the youth varied between areas and changed over time. The youth of the previous period – better schooled and often articulate students and ex-students – continued to provide the core of the formal leadership of youth organisations. As levels of conflict rose, other young people were drawn in. The emergent informal leadership included new faces as well as long-standing leaders, with the criteria for leadership shifting from political articulateness to strategic skills, physical strength or courage. Young people were drawn into 'political' action not only through political conviction, but also because joining the comrades could be fun, provide affirmation in a variety of ways, and even legitimate violent behaviour.

Violence did not involve only the 'unemployed' or those lacking political discipline. Students and others participated, whether out of conviction that this had become a necessary component of the liberation struggle, or because of local political dynamics and conditions. Repressive action by the state, with the 'collaboration' of some township residents, was widely interpreted as violence

---

47 Aggrey Klaaste: 'The lovely kids we turned into monsters', *Frontline*, (September 1985); Seekings: 'A town where 14 year-olds battle police', *Weekly Mail*, 25 April 1986; Collinge, J-A: 'The Teenagers of Tumahole', *Work in Progress* 58 (March/April 1989); Roux: *How Revolutionaries Use Children*.

against the 'community', which had to defend itself with violence. The youth of the mid-1980s cannot be reduced to either disciplined young revolutionaries, or to deviant unemployed louts.

Tensions among the youth

The escalation of conflict and violence drew in a wide range of township residents, but also gave rise to tensions and disputes. Both the prominence of young people and the incidence of violence were widely criticised. Not only did 'generational' tensions sometimes grow, but the youth were also divided among themselves. Considering the heterogeneous character of the youth, this is hardly surprising.

In some cases divisions among the youth were primarily over issues of class and education. In Kagiso there was considerable tension between different youth. The membership of the Kagiso Youth Congress, which the organisation claimed rose to about seven hundred signed-up members, included students, workers and young unemployed people. But in January 1986 a group of unemployed members left the youth congress and formed the breakaway Kagiso United Front. Most of these youth had dropped out of school early on, even before Standard Three. They resented being sneered at by the more educated youth for not being 'learned', and said that they could not participate in meetings which were conducted in English, which few of them could understand well. Kagiso Youth Congress members were reported to have described United Front youth as being dirty because they did not wash.[48]

The incorporation of a wider range of youth into youth organisations, which had hitherto comprised better educated young people, was often a difficult process. The leaders of one of the strongest youth organisations in Natal, the Imbali Youth Organisation, made a conscious effort to form an organisation which could accommodate different young people. The founders had formerly been members of the DCO Matiwane Youth Organisation, which had conducted its meetings in English and came to be seen as an

---

48 See evidence of Dlamini, *Krugersdorp Residents Organisation (KRO) and others vs Minister of Law and Order and others*, pp. 192, 200.

organisation for the children of professionals. The Imbali Youth Organisation, formed in April 1985, attracted a wider range of young people.[49]

Social differences often overlapped with disagreements over tactics and ideology, with more educated student or ex-student leaders in formal leadership positions differing with non-student youth over the role of organisation and discipline within the struggle. In Alexandra, for example, the leadership of Ayco comprised well-educated students, mostly from Cosas backgrounds, but were detained under the State of Emergency from July 1985 to March 1986. In early 1986, while they were still in detention, Alexandra exploded in violent conflict. Youth fought with the police, evicting black police and their families from the township, and set up informal policing and judicial structures. The informal leadership which emerged was less educated, and more confrontational, than the detained leaders. The release from detention of the formal Ayco leaders led to a period of considerable tension between them and the new youth leadership.

In townships across South Africa the young militants drawn into the youth during the period of conflict became 'impatient' with the earlier leadership. In some East Rand townships, when student protests spilled over onto the street and non-students became involved, students complained that their struggles had been 'hijacked' by 'unruly elements'.[50]

It is often difficult to identify the key factors in splits within the youth. In Lamontville, dissident members of the local youth organisation (Malayo) split away in 1986 and formed the rebel Lamontville Youth Congress. This appears to have been partly due to broader tensions within Charterist organisations in Natal, and in part based on a critique of the Malayo leadership as being too 'liberal' or moderate. Tensions between the East London Youth Congress and the Border region of the UDF led to the disaffiliation of the Youth Congress. The East London Youth Organisation, a UDF affiliate, seems to have been a rival group. Tensions

---

49 Interview: M Ndlovu.
50 Information on Alexandra from Charles Carter; he briefly refers to this in 'The Alexandra Rebellion', p. 136; interviews: T Letsoenyo, T Mlonyeni.

persisted within the Youth Congress, whose president was later physically assaulted. These tensions too seem to have been rooted in part in broader, nationwide tensions within the Charterist movement.[51]

Many young people were also drawn into violent conflict between different political groupings, for example UDF and Azapo supporters. Reactionary township-based vigilantes also recruited many of their followers from among younger people. The state sponsored 'Eagles' youth clubs in Orange Free State townships with the apparent objective of recruiting youth into organisations that could rival the radical youth congresses. In Natal, the claimed membership of the Inkatha Youth Brigade rose from 439 000 to 719 000 between 1985 and 1989. The IYB's membership even grew rapidly between 1987 and 1989 when the claimed membership of both Inkatha itself and the Inkatha Women's Brigade was falling.[52]

Rising violence exacerbated tensions within the youth. Many of the people who began to identify themselves with youth organisations during this period employed brutal tactics, sometimes against recalcitrant members of the 'community'. As Swilling writes:

Their anti-social sub-culture and predisposition to use violence to give effect to policy decisions existed uncomfortably alongside the social and communal morality that imbued the ideology of national resistance and their own desire to be re-absorbed into the community.[53]

Tensions between activists in formal organisations and the amorphous youth who came to the fore in violent conflict often developed around consumer boycotts. These boycotts were often the first protests where strategic arguments were advanced in support of enforcing compliance. Even among the ranks of youth

---

51 Interviews: Tsenoli, Dlamini (on Lamontville); UDF Border region, 'Secretarial report to the NEC', 22 February 1985; and interviews, O Monareng, S Njikelana (on East London).
52 The membership figures for Inkatha are from Hassim, S: 'Gender, social location and feminist politics in South Africa', *Transformation* 15 (1991).
53 Swilling: 'Because your yard is too big', p. 4.

activists there were many who believed that the end of liberation did not justify some of the means used to achieve it, or who recognised that brutal enforcement was often counter-productive.

The role and effects of violence are well illustrated through the examples of the West Rand townships of Kagiso and Munsieville. In both areas, student and youth organisations had been relatively active in the early 1980s but had largely collapsed by 1984.[54] In 1984-85 student and youth organisation was weak: a few youth were organised into a 'youth department' in the local civic, the Krugersdorp Residents Organisation. Activities related to International Youth Year were largely organised independently of radical political organisation. In Kagiso the escalation of resistance preceded organisational development, with the former therefore strongly shaping the latter.

The first incident in Kagiso followed a Soweto Day meeting in June 1985. After the meeting, several buildings and vehicles were attacked, looted or burnt. Most participants seem to have been young, and included a high proportion of students. In August, local activists called a consumer boycott. Although it did not succeed, 'the consumer boycott became a reference point for the youth' according to one youth leader. A small but growing number of youth were involved in intermittent attacks on buses, and occasionally buildings, over the following months. 'The youth wanted action', recalls another youth leader. In December, activists again called for a consumer boycott to coincide with boycotts organised across the region.

The second boycott led to the youth becoming involved in 'action', although it was not exactly the action, nor the youth, which had been envisaged. Local youth initially enforced the boycott with some brutality. Local activists said that the youth 'did not belong to any particular organisation'; they were 'hooligans' abusing 'the name of the struggle ... criminal elements who were trying to take advantage of the situation by confiscating people's goods'. The police offered a different view of the youth:

---

54 Most of the evidence used is taken from *KRO vs Minister of Law and Order*, and a series of interviews conducted in 1989-90. See further Seekings: 'From quiescence to people's power'.

Youth Politics in the 1980s

Hulle is die militere vleuel van KRO en dit is hulle taak om toe te sien dat uitvoering gegee word aan KRO se besluite, ten einde KRO in staat te stel om sy doelstellings te verwesenlik (They are the military wing of KRO and it is their task to give effect to KRO's decisions, with the aim of achieving KRO's goals).[55]

Facing the prospect of a conservative backlash, activists were forced to respond to these youth. A 'crime prevention' campaign was organised, involving the apprehension and 're-education' of 'hooligans', together with the confiscation of weapons in raids on shebeens. These responses were, to some extent, successful: intimidation and coercion seemed to diminish, and crime was unusually low. To what extent this was due to organisational responses remains unclear, however, as brutal state repression in January and February 1986 forged unprecedented solidarity within the township against the police, and against white traders in neighbouring Krugersdorp.

State repression in Kagiso and Munsieville socially sanctioned militant and direct action and broadened support for boycotts and other protests. No doubt the former 'hooligans' and 'criminal elements' were at the forefront of attacks on delivery vehicles and clashes with police. Such youth were a large part of the driving force of the struggle, but were also a constant organisational problem at the local level. In Charterist political discourse at the time, young militants were the youth or the 'young lions' when they took on the state, or appeared to be acting in a disciplined manner; but they were 'criminal elements' or 'hooligans' when their actions undermined or challenged township organisation.

There were similar problems with direct action by the 'youth', including violence and theft during consumer boycotts, in many other townships. In the Eastern Cape, consumer boycotts seem to have involved less intimidation and conflict, but Swilling points to some tensions which he attributes to the 'militaristic sub-culture of the *amabutho*'. Soweto's leading boycott organiser denounced *tsotsis* masquerading as comrades; after Soyco members apprehended some such masqueraders the youth congress conducted an

---

55 Affidavit of Brigadier DJ van Wyk, *KRO vs Minister of Law and Order*, p. 56.

Operation 'Root Out Thugs' (which was widely praised, even by the police!). It was at this time that the term *comtsotsis* seems to have become widely used.

In Cape Town, the brutal enforcement of a consumer boycott by youth was a major factor in provoking conservative vigilantes (the *witdoeke*, so-called because of their white head-scarves) into a violent reaction. In a few areas – particularly Soweto – violent clashes took place between youth organisations and local gangs. In parts of Cape Town, Cayco leaders sought to work with gang leaders to curb crime.[56]

'People's courts' also gave rise to 'abuse' by undisciplined youth. In his keynote address to the national education conference in Durban in March 1986, Zwelakhe Sisulu distinguished between 'disciplined, organised youth', who helped to set up accountable 'organs of people's power', and the 'bands of youth' who formed kangaroo courts. Scharf and Ngcokoto analysed the transformation of a people's court in Nyanga East (in Cape Town) in late 1985. The court, under the influence of active and long-standing members of local youth organisations, was initially concerned with democratic practice and prefigurative justice. But the court was gradually taken over by other youth – the 'marginalised' youth, according to Scharf and Ngcokoto – who had either been recruited during violent confrontations with the police, or who had been brought before the court to be disciplined and rehabilitated. The new youth clashed with the court's earlier leaders from local youth organisations. Punishments became increasingly brutal, procedures became grotesque, and the court rapidly lost support.[57]

---

56 Murray, M: *South Africa: Time of Agony, Time of Destiny* (London: Verso, 1987), pp. 308-15; Roux, A and Helliker, K: *Voices from Rini: A Survey of Black Attitudes towards a Consumer Boycott in Grahamstown*, Rhodes University, Institute for Social and Economic Research, working paper 23, 1986; Swilling: 'Because your yard is too big', p. 5; *City Press*, 12 August 1985, 25 August 1985, 27 October 1985, 24 November 1985; *Star* and *Sowetan*, 28 October 1985; *South* 30 July 1987; Obery, I and Jochelson, K: 'Consumer Boycotts', *Work in Progress* 39 (October 1985).

57 Sisulu, Z: 'People's Education for People's Power', *Transformation* 1 (1986), pp. 104-6; Scharf, W and Ngcokoto, B: 'Images of punishment in the people's courts of Cape Town', 1985-7', in Manganyi and Du Toit (eds): *Political Violence and the Struggle in South Africa*

The enforcement of stayaways in many areas raised issues of class. Workers stood to lose income during stayaways, and were sometimes not persuaded by the arguments advanced for particular actions. In the Eastern Cape, trade unions and workers clashed with the youth, both verbally and physically, over stayaways in early and mid-1985.[58]

Disagreements also surfaced, both among young people and between them and older residents, over school boycotts. In many townships, students were divided over the continuation of school boycotts. Some students sought to keep boycotts going, by force if necessary. Many parents were opposed to continued school boycotts, and in some townships tried to escort their children to school. Many parents' committees were formed to conclude boycotts by mediating between, and negotiating with, school authorities and students. These led to the formation of the Soweto Parents Crisis Committee in December 1985, and the National Education Crisis Committee in 1986.[59]

Many older people felt that younger people were playing inappropriate roles. This was clearly based on a certain amount of 'generational' tension. As Mokwena put it: 'In the process of violent struggle, the youth developed a noticeable arrogance which resulted in intense generational conflict between youth and elders ...'[60] Older people witnessed the very first direct action, in the Vaal Uprising, with mixed feelings. According to a 'middle-aged man' from Sebokeng in the Vaal Triangle:

> *Sebokeng was sliding dangerously close to anarchy. We found bands of youths being a law unto themselves ... Everyone here is angry with the way our affairs are administered. Our rents*

(Halfway House: Southern Books, 1990); Burman, S and Scharf, W: 'Creating people's justice: street committees and people's courts in South Africa', *Law and Society Review* 24/3 (1990).

58 Pillay, D: 'The Port Elizabeth stayaway', *Work in Progress* 37 (June 1985); Adler, G: 'Uniting a community', *Work in Progress* 50 (October/November 1987).

59 See Straker: *Faces in the Revolution*, p. 26; *Sowetan*, 21 October 1984; Muller, J: 'People's education and the National Education Crisis Committee', *South African Review 4*.

60 Mokwena: 'Living on the wrong side of the law', p. 37.

are among the highest ... But I do not like the way the whole thing has been taken over by our children ... Some of them did not know what the fighting was all about.[61]

The operation of people's courts was frequently controversial. While their effectiveness in containing crime was generally welcomed, their procedures and practices were questioned and opposed. In many townships older residents resented young people arbitrating in marital and other disputes, and opposed the brutality of the sentences. In some areas, the militancy of the 'youth' made local activists wary of intervening. 'The youth become uncontrollable at times', Alexandra leaders said; the leaders realised that 'a certain bad element amongst the youth' might assault anyone who dared to criticise them.[62]

Just as 'people's education' was as much a response to disorderly students as it was to the shortcomings of apartheid education, so the formation of people's courts and street committees was a response to the unruliness of the youth, as much as to the collapse and illegitimacy of state administration. Lodge writes that in Port Elizabeth, 'street committees headed by elders were seen by UDF officials as the best means to ensure that the monitoring of the [consumer] boycott did not rest with self-appointed youthful leaders.'[63]

It should not be thought that there was general hostility between older and younger residents. Indeed, much of the militancy and even violence of the 'youth' was validated or legitimated by the approval of other residents.[64] Student protesters enjoyed the support of many parents,[65] and the involvement of young people and the use of violence in civic protests was widely supported.

Generational conflict, where it existed, was most pronounced in rural areas, particularly in the Eastern Transvaal and Natal/KwaZulu. Ritchken's work in the Eastern Transvaal shows

---

61 *Sunday Star*, 28 October 1984.
62 Seekings: 'People's courts and popular politics', *South African Review 5* (Johannesburg: Ravan, 1989).
63 Lodge and Nasson: *All, Here and Now*, p. 82.
64 See for example Straker: *Faces in the Revolution*, p. 103.
65 See for example *Sunday Star*, 28 October 1984 on the Vaal Triangle and *Evening Post*, 14 March 1984 on Cradock.

how, in the absence of adult male migrants, major struggles over resources developed between older women and young, largely unemployed people. One extreme result of this was the killing of alleged witches – generally older women. In Natal/KwaZulu generational tensions seem to have been one factor which fueled violent conflict in areas which historically had been strongly patriarchal.[66]

Violence and the marginalisation of young women

A range of factors combined to draw very different people into violence in the mid-1980s: national political consciousness and local political conditions, together with opportunities for 'fun', gain or building self-esteem and social recognition. But one major category of young people tended to be marginalised, in terms of both organisation and action, as township politics became increasingly violent. This group was young women.

Women were prominently involved in civic struggles in the early and mid-1980s. Many young women were also involved in youth organisation prior to the outbreak of violent conflict. The leadership of youth organisations was almost entirely male – by a ratio of about six to one in the case of the first four youth congresses set up in the PWV region in 1983-84 – but a much higher proportion of the active membership involved women. Young women comprised almost one-third of the seventy-one 'youths' identified as active in the Alexandra Youth Congress (prior to the outbreak of violence in Alexandra in 1986), and almost one half of the initial one hundred members of the Tumahole Youth Congress formed in January 1985.[67] Of the sixty-odd youth who fled from

---

66 Ritchken, E: 'Burning the herbs: Youth politics and witches in Lebowa', *Work in Progress* 48 (July 1987); 'Comrades, witches and the state: the case of the Brooklyn Youth Organisation', paper presented to the African Studies seminar, University of the Witwatersrand, September 1987; Kentridge: *An Unofficial War.*
67 On Alexandra, see Carter: 'We are the Progressives'; on Tumahole, see Seekings: 'Political mobilisation in Tumahole'.

Leandra (whom Straker later studied), nineteen were women.

The age profile of the women involved in these youth organisations differed strikingly from that of the male members. Three-quarters of the women in Ayco were aged eighteen years or under, in contrast to just one-fifth of the male members. The female members of Ayco were mostly of school-going age, and most were in fact students, while the male members were older, most having completed their secondary schooling. Similarly, in Tumahole, the female members of the Youth Congress were mostly students who had been prominently involved in school protests the previous year.

Why, then, were women rarely prominent in the youth during the violent confrontations of the mid-1980s? Township politics has generally been characterised by discriminatory ideologies about gender roles, but in conditions of violence men develop or adopt even more discriminatory gender ideologies. Fighting – and indeed 'political' activity in general – came to be seen (by men, at least) as a matter for men alone. They often explained the absence or exclusion of women with reference to the alleged inability of women to keep secrets, both in public and especially under interrogation by police. This seems to be a very dubious assertion. Men also pointed to the burden of domestic chores on women – forgetting that this had not previously prevented women from being involved in civic and educational protests, and in youth organisation.[68]

Women were involved in some incidents, however, including the killing of Skhosana in Duduza (discussed above). Women were drawn into such transient participation in the 'youth' in the same way as men, primarily as a result of the local political conditions which seemed to require the defence of the 'community'. The case of Skhosana was an extreme one, as the whole incident was steeped in sexual symbolism: not only was the victim a woman herself, but the 'evidence' that she was a sell-out was that she was (allegedly) a girlfriend of a local policeman.

Women were drawn into sustained violent action only rarely. The profiles which Straker provides from Leandra seem to confirm

---

68 Seekings: 'Gender ideology and township politics in the 1980s', *Agenda* 10 (1991).

this. Straker suggests that 'Pretty', for example, had been drawn into attending meetings and other activities by her boyfriend:

> *[Her boyfriend] was very guarded about his activities, in which he was careful not to involve Pretty if he thought they could be dangerous. If, for example, he thought that there might be trouble at a meeting, he would forbid her to attend and beat her if she did.*

Straker describes one incident in which Pretty was loosely involved:

> *[Pretty] was walking with her boyfriend and six others near the outskirts of the township when they saw the van, which had broken down. The boys decided after a brief discussion to attack it. Pretty was instructed to wait where she was, out of harm's way but to observe.*

Pretty was afterwards called on to help remove the food that was in the van. Straker writes that Pretty saw her boyfriend's restrictions as protective not abusive.[69]

Campbell seems to suggest that rising violence and the assertion of male dominance were closely linked, rooted in the 'crisis of masculinity'. The implication is that, as male youth came to define themselves as fighters and protectors of the home, they relegated women to the role of nurturers in the home.[70]

Summary

During the mid-1980s the category of youth was once again reconstructed in the face of burgeoning resistance to the state. In the previous period, from 1976 through the early 1980s, the youth emerged in the form of the graduates of 1976: educated, politically articulate and committed to working for political change outside of the workplace and the school. They included both men and

---

69 Straker: *Faces in the Revolution*, p. 55-6.
70 Campbell: 'Learning to kill?'.

women.

In the mid-1980s the definition of what kinds of activity were 'political' expanded, with the youth including a much wider range and larger number of people. Local youth organisations proliferated, and a national structure was eventually formed in 1987. The youth included street-fighters and more strategic exponents of violence, conformists who enjoyed the camaraderie and fun of toyi-toying (and more) with the comrades, and a wide range of people who were transiently drawn into brief incidents of violence against the enemies of the 'community'. The heterogeneity of the youth led to tensions within the youth, as well as between them and others. These tensions concerned social or class differences, as well as tactical and organisational differences.

Finally, during this period of violent conflict, women were largely marginalised within the youth.

Chapter Four

Youth in transition, 1988-92

In townships and rural areas throughout South Africa, large numbers of people were drawn into the youth during the conflict of the mid-1980s. These many and different youth have not moved in any single direction since then, but in many. The political context has involved many and complex changes: escalating repression under the State of Emergency, the revival of defiance in 1989, the unbanning of the ANC and other organisations and dissolution of old organisations such as the United Democratic Front, the onset of negotiations, and rising political violence. Many youth have stayed within the ranks of youth organisation, but more have left. Some of these have drifted into – or, in many cases, returned to – life on the margins of legality.

The slow and uneven transition away from apartheid has been characterised by high levels of violence. This has included political violence, continuing from the 1980s in Natal/KwaZulu and starting up anew on the Reef since July 1990. Together with the high levels of crime and the continuing crisis in black schooling, this fueled discussion in the media of the anarchic, undisciplined, 'lost generation'.

Evidence on these issues is sketchy, reflecting the paucity of existing studies. Research currently under way by other scholars will throw more light on this important topic.[1]

Organisation: from Sayco to the Youth League

The key organisational development during this period involved the transformation of Sayco and its component youth congresses into a relaunched ANC Youth League and branches. This was preceded, however, by other important initiatives. Youth leaders played a prominent part in the revival of resistance politics in general, and of youth organisations in particular.

With the revival of opposition politics in 1989-90, Sayco emerged from hiding. This was not an easy transition. Major debates were waged over Sayco's federal structure (which was more appropriate in the earlier repressive conditions), an alleged lack of democracy and consultation in decision making and of accountability of leadership, and its relationship with the ANC.

Many of these issues were raised at Sayco's first national congress, held in Kangwane over the Easter weekend of April 1990. As Sayco's new publicity secretary admitted, 'Congress came up with a number of lessons for us'. The conference involved an unprecedented number of youth activists: nearly two thousand delegates represented the ten existing regions and the new Transkei region. The opening address was given by recently released ANC leader, Nelson Mandela.[2]

The future of Sayco dominated the conference, particularly whether it should merge with the ANC's Youth Section and form a revived ANC Youth League. The Sayco leadership had already met with ANC leaders in Lusaka at least twice (August/September 1989 and early April 1990), and seemed to have reached an agreement – in principle at least – to merge. No decision was reached at the conference, although it was resolved that Sayco should adopt a unitary structure, which would facilitate any subsequent merger. The new unitary structure involved the reconstitution of the local

---

1   See the various research reports issued by C A S E, on behalf of the Joint Enrichment Project, dealing with a range of youth-related issues.
2   See Niddrie, D: 'Sayco eyes the ANC', *Work In Progress* 65 (April 1990), p. 2; and 'Sayco: Now just a phone call away', *Work In Progress* 66 (May 1990), pp. 2-4.

youth congresses as branches. Following the conference Sayco held meetings in each region (including a new, twelfth region in the Western Transvaal) to discuss issues raised, particularly the future role of youth organisation and relations with an unbanned ANC now involved in negotiations.[3]

Conference resolutions included one calling for the 'phasing out' of the UDF, shifting the political role to the ANC; and supporting negotiations with 'maximum mobilisation and organisation of our people'. Perhaps the most important, with hindsight, was a resolution strongly denouncing Inkatha leader Mangosuthu Buthelezi, and calling for the formation of defence units. Sayco was at the forefront of attempts to campaign against violence in Natal/KwaZulu on a national basis, and in isolating Inkatha. The campaign against Inkatha was accompanied by attacks on Inkatha leaders' houses in parts of the Transvaal, further contributing to the rising tensions which boiled over with the massive, hostel-centered violence on the Reef from July 1990.

Sayco's restructuring was important not only because it facilitated a merger with the ANC Youth Section, but also because it implicitly recognised some of Sayco's past weaknesses. Sayco's federal structure had enabled it to draw in a huge membership. But it had also inhibited the development of organisation and discipline, and of political education within Sayco structures. Sayco itself noted this:

> *The reality of the situation is that ... it has been easy for the youth to identify with [youth structures] in the process of struggle ... [T]hroughout the country youth congresses would consider themselves as part of Sayco. However ... there wouldn't be a precise understanding as to where and how they should take forward Sayco's programmes.*[4]

A unitary structure was seen as a means of facilitating communication and uniform action. Sayco's national education committee reported in May 1990 on the 'shocking' state of political education

---

3   *Work in Progress* 66; *Weekly Mail*, 20 April 1990; *New Nation*, 15 September 1989, 5 April 1990.
4   Sayco: 'Towards restructuring and transforming Sayco into a unitary structure', p. 3.

in the regions. There was 'no structured – let alone consistent – political education of youth activists – both at local, zonal and regional levels', and there were 'very few areas where education structures exist, again from local, regional to national level'.[5]

The ANC Youth League was relaunched in October 1990, marking the merger of the exile-based Youth Section with Sayco. The Youth League's leadership included former Sayco leaders in key positions, including Peter Mokaba as president. Provisional youth committees were established at regional and branch level to prepare the revival of Youth League structures. As the ANC magazine *Mayibuye* reported, the Youth League faced the difficult task of balancing a tradition of militancy with support for the ANC's chosen tactic of negotiations. Many youth were suspicious of negotiations, as an earlier article in *Mayibuye* had noted: 'Simply put, young lions were steeped in the politics of opposition that excluded debate with their enemy.' For the ANC, the participation and support of such youth was both a major asset and a potential liability; some of the most prominent (and outspokenly militant) Youth League leaders were regarded with wariness by other ANC leaders.[6]

The different regions of the Youth League were launched from mid-1991 onwards. The PWV region was the first to be launched, in May, with 35 000 paid-up members. The region with the largest membership at the time of its launch seems to have been Eastern Transvaal, with 37 000 members. The Eastern Cape region had surprisingly few members ('over' ten thousand, only); the Western Cape was also described as 'weak', with only 7 500 members.[7]

The membership of the ANC Youth League was much lower than the membership claimed by Sayco and its affiliates in the late 1980s. The membership of the Eastern Cape was one-tenth of that claimed by the Sayco region in 1987. One explanation was given by a Port Elizabeth Youth League leader, who complained that the

---

5   Minutes of Sayco national education committee meeting, Cape Town, 29-30 May 1990, p. 10.
6   'A home for the youth', *Mayibuye* (December 1990), pp. 40-42; 'Learning to trust tactics of talks', *Mayibuye* (September 1990), pp. 33-35.
7   *Horizon* 2 (May/June 1991), 3 (July/August 1991) and 4 (October 1991).

formation of the League had been 'a dull, slow process, which has failed to capture the mood and imagination of the youth'. In addition, the transition from Sayco to the Youth League had been very 'chaotic and unco-ordinated'.[8]

Youth and violence

What has happened to the youth of the mid-1980s? Where are they now? Straker's study of youth from Leandra provides some insight. In 1989 Straker tracked down some of the youth activists whom she had interviewed in 1986. She found that the youth had responded very differently to their earlier experiences of brutal and sustained violence in 1985-86. Some had coped well. This was especially true of the leaders, several of whom had been politicised within their families, and whose parents had often been supportive:

> *Their values were learned in the intimacy of the home. They were taught directly and role models were immediately available. They were not inducted primarily by the peer group, as were many of the others.*[9]

Youth who were mobilised through formal or informal political education, and whose educators (whether parents or otherwise) served as role models, were more likely to cope with violence experienced in the struggle. Straker identifies another group who seem to have been little affected by their experiences of violence:

> *There are vast numbers of youth who in 1984-86 were carried along [on] the tide of emotion and the whirlwind liberation struggle that swept the country, but have now returned their energies to living out their lives in a more mundane context.*

One example of this is 'Pretty': 'In retrospect', according to Straker, 'Pretty's participation in the struggle during 1984-86 seems in many ways to have been an incidental one; a ripple on

---

8   *Horizon* 4 (October 1991), p. 14.
9   Straker: *Faces in the Revolution*, p. 85.

the stream of her life despite the momentous events it encompassed.'[10] Straker emphasises the psychological resilience of the youth, many of whom have coped well with chronic stress.

Research by other psychologists supports the view that there is no necessary relationship between exposure to and subsequent acceptance of violence. Even children who have been exposed to violence are not predisposed to use violence themselves. Dawes and others report that children distinguish between different forms of violence, endorsing 'political' more than 'non-political' (eg domestic) violence. It seems to be more the nature of the violence which children experience, and its context, rather than exposure of violence itself, which shapes their attitudes to violence.[11] This contrasts with the conventional wisdom that children are socialised into violent behaviour.[12]

But some of the youth Straker discusses have coped less well. Many had been socialised not by older role models, but by their peer group, not through political education but through political conflict. Straker provides the example of 'Len', who had a history of violent outbursts, and had become a heavy user of drugs and alcohol. Since 1986 he had become angry and morose, resentful of authority in general and of whites in particular. He had also become a leading member among local *tsotsis*. These largely unemployed gang members

> are nostalgic for the good old days of excitement and action when their own positions and roles were more clearly defined. They show an inability to return to mundane lives, to forge a new identity for themselves within their changed circumstances.'[13]

---

10 Straker: *Faces in the Revolution*, p. 60.
11 Dawes, A: 'The effects of political violence on children', *International Journal of Psychology* 25 (1990); Pastor, C: 'Children and Attitudes to Violence: Effects of Exposure to Political Violence', Honours thesis, University of Cape Town (1988).
12 See Klaaste, 'The lovely kids we turned into monsters'; also *SA Pressclips*, 'Youth and the Future' (supplement) December 1990, pp. 6-12.
13 Straker: *Faces in the Revolution*, p. 81.

There appear to be many youth in the same position as Len.

Many townships are reported to have suffered from youth violence which has turned against the 'community'. In Witbank, for example, some of the comrades from 1984-86 formed a gang which harassed and stole from township residents. In Khutsong, on the far West Rand, former 'comrades' formed the 'Gaddafis' gang; scores were reported killed in clashes with the rival 'Zim-Zims'. Khutsong residents criticised both gangs. In Bekkersdal, also on the West Rand, conflict between ANC, Azapo and Inkatha-aligned youth escalated when local gangs joined in the fray. In Sebokeng, in the Vaal Triangle, former comrades were reported to be assisting Inkatha in violent attacks on ANC leaders. In Khayelitsha, former comrades have turned to crime and are alleged to have shot at and even killed local ANC and civic leaders.[14]

Mokwena, in his analysis of the growth of violent youth gangs in Soweto, attributes the rise of these gangs to 'material and structural deprivation': unemployment and poverty, the disintegration of township schooling, and the experience of violence in the mid-1980s which resulted in the transformation of hierarchies of authority both within the youth and within the family or community. Gangs provided a social framework in which theft, violence and rape are legitimate, even virtuous.[15] Cape Town is another area with a continuing gang problem, with police estimating that one hundred thousand people are involved in gangs in one way or another.[16]

In a second article, Mokwena focuses on 'jackrolling' – the violent abduction and rape of young women – which he sees as an extreme manifestation of the more general gang problem. Building

---

14 Interview: D Mdluli; Koch, E and Blecher, S: 'Laying down the law, Toughman- style', *Weekly Mail*, 15 February 1991; Garson, P: 'Thugs rule the "no-go" zone', *Weekly Mail*, 12 April 1991; Garson, P: 'In this senseless hell, death is a way of life', *Weekly Mail*, 8 February 1991; Koch, E and Blecher, S: 'Youth "comtsotsis": can the ANC ride the tiger?', *Weekly Mail*, 8 February 1991; '"Comtsotsi" reign of township terror', *Argus,* 6-7 February 1993.
15 Mokwena: 'Living on the wrong side of the law'. See a gangster's view in 'Rapist? not me, says the "jackroller"', *Weekly Mail*, 6 September 1991.
16 'Gangs thrive in miasma', *Weekly Mail,* 11 January 1991.

on his earlier paper, Mokwena argues that structural factors led to the marginalisation of black youth, in primarily economic terms. This produced a violent and 'survivalistic' youth culture, which revolves around the need to 'get by', through exploiting the environment for resources. Violence and machismo characterise this culture. Many of these gang members had been comrades in the mid-1980s, and before that *tsotsis*.[17]

Mokwena warns against romanticising the youth. Gangs in Soweto have had a hostile relationship with political organisations. Mokwena writes that gangs do not 'exist on the fringes of the political movement, [but] instead they often serve to actively obstruct rather than enhance its objectives.' Cosas and Soweto Youth Congress activists killed, and were killed, in clashes with gangs. In other areas (including the South-eastern Transvaal), Inkatha or the security forces seem to have recruited among gangs, provided training, and then set these youth against the ANC and allied civic groups.

Escalating political conflict – especially on the Reef since July 1990 – provided conditions in which many youth could again become involved in 'legitimate' violence. A survey of township residents on the Reef in early 1991 found that large numbers of people identified 'youths or pseudo-comrades' as the people mainly responsible for starting the violence in their area. This was alleged by about one-third of the respondents from Pretoria and Soweto, slightly fewer on the East Rand, but almost half on the West Rand. (Only on the West Rand – where there had been little violence – did more people identify the youth than Inkatha as being primarily responsible for violence).

Gangs and youth have been a chronic problem in both Soweto and the Vaal Triangle. In late May 1992 the *Weekly Mail* sensationally (but not inaccurately) wrote of Soweto:

> *While an uprising like that of 1976 seems unlikely, aimless revolts by gun-toting 1990s youths, unemployed and hardened*

---

17 Mokwena: 'The era of the jackrollers: contextualising the rise of youth gangs in Soweto', Project for the Study of Violence seminar paper no. 7, University of the Witwatersrand, October 1991. See also Cross, M: 'Youth culture and resistance in South Africa', *Perspectives in Education* 12/2 (1991), pp. 41- 42; *Weekly Mail* 23 March 1990.

> by the factional violence of the past two years, may be a lot worse. Already anarchic, misplaced violence is part of township life.

In regard to the Vaal Triangle, it was claimed that:

> The revolt of township youths in the Vaal is already uglier than the uprisings of June 1976. Today's youths are armed, their violence anarchic and random, their targets innocent passers-by.

On the East Rand, '*tsotsi comrades*' were reported to have seized control of the Phola Park squatter camp, driving out the former civic leaders.[18] Such behaviour fueled fears, including among ANC and Sayco leaders, that the youth were not adjusting well to the new politics of negotiations. Walter Sisulu admitted as early as 1990 that:

> It's not easy for us to sit down to negotiate. The problem is many of the youngsters are not really interested in the negotiations. In fact they've become a little bit angry. That is why I say that this chap De Klerk is moving too fast and can create problems for us.[19]

Former UDF leader Murphy Morobe elaborated:

> For many of the youth, the struggle has meant simply to shoot your way to Pretoria ... We acknowledge that the degree of political education has not been commensurate with the degree and extent of political mobilisation that we have been able to generate. And that brings to the fore an important and serious contradiction. You draw in to the movement battalions and battalions of young lions, hearts in the right place, determined to become part of the struggle, but often they don't understand the basic political positions of the movement.[20]

---

18 'Frustrated youths fight a faceless foe', *Weekly Mail*, 29 May 1992; 'It's worse than '76', *Weekly Mail*, 29 May 1992; 'Putsch of the tsotsi comrades', *Weekly Mail*, 10 April 1992.
19 'Slow down, FW. We still have to educate our people', *Weekly Mail*, 26 January 1990.

In some respects, the patterns of violence in 1990-92 are similar to those of 1984-86. However, whereas in the past violence was seen in terms of the political struggle, now it is seen more as a problem in itself.[21] But the patterns have not changed. Many young people have been drawn into violence, through both township-based self-defence units, reactionary vigilante groups or hostel-based impis.

But not all violence can be attributed to young people. A wide range of township residents and squatters have been involved in the violence – acting in defence of townships against invading impis, and in retaliatory action. And, just as in the mid-1980s, there appears to be a low level of national political consciousness, but a high level of local political consciousness on the part of participants.

---

20 'Slow down, FW. We still have to educate our people', *Weekly Mail*, 26 January 1990.
21 See Du Toit, A: 'Understanding South African Political Violence: a new problematic?', paper presented at UNRISD workshop, Geneva, May 1992.

Chapter Five

Conclusion and prospects

This study has focused on the youth as just one section of the population of young people in South Africa's townships. This section of the population has been defined and understood not in demographic or sociological terms, but according to forms of behaviour and the attitudes imputed to the participants. As these forms of behaviour became more or less common, and as the context changed, so the category of youth has changed in size, composition and character.

In the mid-1970s few people were organised into overtly political youth organisations. The protesters in 1976 were generally identified as students, although acts of violence were widely attributed to the amorphous youth. It was only in the aftermath of 1976-77 that the category of youth came to be recognised by the ANC and its allies. The challenge facing them was to ensure that students remained politically active after the revolts had declined. The core of the youth in the 1979-84 period was to comprise the ex-student activists, who were seen as politically engaged, not via educational or workplace struggles, but directly against the state. These youth were articulate, and highly politicised. They were generally the successes, and not the failures, of the schooling system.

Conclusion and prospects

The category of youth went through a profound transformation – involving both growth and change – during the mid-decade period of township revolt and conflict. Even in 1984 there were relatively few youth, in the sense that there were few overtly political youth congresses, and these had a small membership. By 1987 the South African Youth Congress claimed a signed-up membership of half-a-million, and a support base of two million. The claimed signed-up membership alone was probably between fifty and one hundred times the membership of similar youth organisations in the early 1980s.

This growth occurred because large numbers of people were politicised through their experience of conflict. Many were drawn into forms of direct action including a range of acts and types of violence. Escalating conflict opened up new spaces for gang members, among others. This was a period when there was widespread celebration of violence and machismo.

The ANC encouraged almost any form of militancy as contributing to the intensifying 'people's war' against the state, in which the youth were the heroic combatants. Direct action and confrontation also provided spaces for a range of people to seek social affirmation, and even to enjoy themselves through collective action. The intensification of local struggles drew many people into conflict, including violent conflict, who would otherwise have remained passive or peaceful. Young women, by contrast, were largely marginalised.

The numbers of youth thus grew rapidly in the mid-1980s. They were politicised, but the term was broadened to embrace anyone defying the state rather than the former understanding in terms of ideological clarity. The broadening of the concept of the youth generated many tensions, both within the youth and between them and other people. Some tensions revolved around social class or educational differences; others around tactical or organisational differences. Many involved disagreements over the degree of militancy accompanying particular tactics or campaigns. The tension between harnessing and controlling militancy lay beneath these disagreements: the cause of liberation through struggle could be furthered by diverse people in disparate ways, but some of these people and methods repeatedly threatened to turn against the community rather than the state.

Following the repression of the late 1980s the composition of the youth has changed once again. Understanding the heterogeneity and fluidity of the youth helps us understand how the youth have moved in different directions since the mid-1980s. A small proportion of the youth of the 1980s have moved into structures such as the ANC Youth League. But many have not remained organisationally active, finding the transition into the youth wing of a political party unappealing. Another section of the youth have continued their activities of the mid-1980s but with (as had been feared) other members of the 'community' replacing the state as the target and victim. Many youth have been demobilised.

This short study has emphasised that, since the mid-1970s, the youth have comprised neither a monolithic nor a static category of people. Bundy and others have suggested that there is a 'distinctive' youth contribution to resistance. However, if we define the youth in terms of militancy or violence (and related behavioral and psychological characteristics), it becomes meaningless to conclude that the youth are distinctively militant. This would be akin to stating that militant people are distinctively militant, or that violent people are distinctively violent.

Are young people distinctively militant, politicised or involved in violence? This remains unclear. Young people clearly played a central role in many protests, and young people initiated or led protests or violent conflicts in many cases. But is there a clear contrast between the attitudes or actions of younger and older people? Bundy (among others) suggests that a generational consciousness was forged during the early and mid-1980s. He points out that such consciousness is most easily created at a critical historical conjuncture such as a period of major societal change. The mid-1980s provided such a conjuncture, which people experienced directly through violent conflict.

Many of the youth contrasted their militancy with their parents' passivity. But this self-perception did not in itself constitute a pervasive generational consciousness. A range of pointers suggest that young people had – and have – diverse views, that a large number are as politically conservative as their parents, and that only a minority of young people participated in those forms of direct action

Conclusion and prospects

we associate with militancy.

Unfortunately, there has not been enough research into experiences and attitudes of the full range of young people in South Africa allow strong conclusions about the significance of age. But the changing size and composition of the youth should alert us to the problems of providing a general account of, for example, 'youth culture', or a general catch-all explanation of 'youth' behaviour. There seem to be diverse 'youth cultures' – differing by region and period, and between different groups of youth in the same time and place – and there are further cultures associated with young people outside of the youth.

We began by suggesting that the youth have generally been understood in terms of either violence or politicisation. As we have seen, however, these categories of 'violence' and 'politicisation' are as fluid and ambiguous as the category of youth itself. The link between youth and violence posits violence as senseless or irresponsible behaviour; its connotations are negative, particularly in regard to destruction. But violence often involves actors behaving with cool rationality, many of whom are older or otherwise fall outside of our understanding of 'youth'. Violence also occurs in patterns which reveal considerable order, reflecting the contours of justice and morality in local political culture (more than opportunism, random barbarism or conspiratorial organisation).

Similarly, we can ask what 'politicisation' means? Does it involve a conscious commitment to a clearly articulated and understood political ideology? Or does it mean behaving in ways which can be interpreted as political, regardless of motivation? Confronting the state may be political, but those confronting the state are not necessarily politicised.

The fundamental ambiguity of the concept of youth and the prevalence of stereotypes in the South African context raises many problems for political analysis. Perhaps the concept of youth needs to be put aside. Subsequent research into the politics of young people in South Africa should not take the category of youth as its starting point, but rather seek to identify and analyse the political attitudes, preferences, organisations and activities (or inactivity) of all young South Africans.

It remains important, nonetheless, to bear in mind these characterisations of youth in terms of violence and politicisation. The latter characterisation, at least, informed the self-perception of many of the youth. And it contributed to many of the persistent features of youth behaviour. One reason for the repeated delays before the formation of regional and national youth structures was the ideological and organisational conflicts among the youth. These were associated with different groups' understandings of how to implement their 'political' mission. The centrality of politics to their self-understanding underlay the scale of conflicts over the interpretation or application of politics. Similarly, the centrality of politics underlay political intolerance, including the use of direct action (including killing) against people identified as counter-revolutionary.

The youth of the 1980s comprised a very heterogeneous and changing section of the population. What they had in common – by definition – was an involvement in political action, and especially direct action. Many of the youth of the 1980s are no longer youth, having ceased to be involved in such activity. Many, or even most, young people are not among the youth today. But there are nonetheless many youth in South Africa whose attitudes and behaviour are not conducive to stability. As senior officials in organisations like Sayco and the ANC have recognised, some youth were hostile to negotiations, and many former 'comrades' have continued to challenge forms of authority. Much of the current concern about the youth in South Africa arises from the perception that they have remained militant, or violent, while the supposed 'political' motivation for militancy has been superseded by political developments.

The confusion between age and action inherent in the term 'youth' is often understood to mean that there is a generation of young people who are somehow 'lost', whose experiences of unemployment, lack of schooling, and above all confrontation and power in township streets can be aggregated into a single overall problem of the 'youth'. Our analysis of the 1980s, while limited by the readily available sources, suggests that we should be wary of exaggerating the 'youth problem'. The youth, let alone all young people, are far from being monolithic. We must take care to

Conclusion and prospects

specify how many young people are affected by any particular 'problem', and who they are.

Young people in South Africa face many problems, each with serious implications for society as well as the individuals affected: poor economic growth and job creation, hence high unemployment; poor schooling; few recreational facilities; a continued lack of political representation. But most of these are problems shared with older people. They are not problems which can be equated with the youth.

Just as young people and the youth as categories are heterogeneous, so solutions to these problems must be multi-faceted. This study has sought to show that the category of youth – and hence the behaviour of people who are thereby categorised as youth – is in large part contingent on the context. The context thus needs to be addressed. A political settlement, which includes establishing a legitimate system of enforcing law and order, will remove much of the political content to the youth. At the time of his release in 1990, Nelson Mandela stated that, if the National Party government created the necessary conditions, the ANC and allied organisations would be successfully able to 'appeal to the youth to discipline themselves, go back to school and concentrate on their studies.'[1]

But will the young lions be so easily tamed? Mandela's view ignores other aspects of the youth. Many youth no doubt do have great expectations of a post-apartheid South Africa. Some of these can presumably be met with relative ease. For example, the provision of basic recreational facilities would provide an alternative to street-based action. But other expectations will be beyond the ability of any post-apartheid government to meet. Many youth in South Africa will continue to be unemployed, regardless of the quality of their education. There will continue to be considerable potential for widespread gang activity. Any future government will, in short, face major social challenges. But these factors will, even when taken together, constitute much less than a 'lost generation'.

---

1 *Sunday Star*, 18 February 1990.

Select bibliography

Bundy, Colin: 'Street sociology and pavement politics: some aspects of student/youth consciousness during the 1985 schools crisis in Greater Cape Town', *Journal of Southern African Studies* 13/3 (April 1987).
Campbell, Catherine: 'Learning to kill? Masculinity, the family and violence in Natal', *Journal of Southern African Studies* 18/3 (September 1992).
Carter, Charles: '"We are the progressives": Alexandra Youth Congress activists and the Freedom Charter, 1983-85', *Journal of Southern African Studies* 17/2 (June 1991).
Cross, Michael: 'Youth culture and resistance in South Africa', *Perspectives in Education* 12/2 (Winter 1991).
Diseko, Nosipho: 'Student Organisation and the Education Struggle in South Africa, 1979-85', paper presented at a conference on Economic Change, Social Conflict and Education in Contemporary South Africa, Grantham, UK, March 1989.
Everatt, David and Sisulu, Elinor (eds): *Black Youth in Crisis: facing the future* (Johannesburg, Ravan Press, 1992).
Gultig, John and Hart, M: '"The world is full of blood": Youth, schooling and conflict in Pietermaritzburg, 1987-1989', *Perspectives in Education* 11/2 (1990).
Hyslop, Jonathan: 'Student school movements and state education policy, 1972-87', in Cobbett, William and Cohen, Robin (eds): *Popular Struggles in South Africa Today* (London: James Currey, 1988).
Johnson, Shaun: 'The Soldiers of Luthuli: Youth in the Politics of Resistance in South Africa', in Johnson, Shaun (ed): *South Africa: No Turning Back* (London: Macmillan, 1988).
Kentridge, Matthew: *An Unofficial War: Inside the Conflict in Pietermaritzburg* (Cape Town: David Philip, 1990).
Lodge, Tom: *All, Here and Now: Black Politics in South Africa in the 1980s* (New York and Cape Town: Ford Foundation and

David Philip, 1991).
Matona, Tshediso: 'Student Organisation and Political Resistance in South Africa: An Analysis of the Congress of South African Students, 1979-1985', Honours dissertation, University of Cape Town (February 1992).
Mokwena, Steve: 'Living on the wrong side of the law: marginalisation, youth and violence', in Everatt, David and Sisulu, Sheila (eds): *Black Youth in Crisis: facing the future* (Johannesburg: Ravan, 1992).
Mokwena, Steve: 'The era of the jackrollers: contextualising the rise of youth gangs in Soweto', Project for the Study of Violence seminar paper no. 7, University of the Witwatersrand (October 1991).
Moller, Valerie: 'Lost Generation Found: Black Youth at Leisure', *Indicator SA*, 'Issue Focus' (May 1991).
Naidoo, Kumi: 'The Politics of Youth Resistance in the 1980s', *Journal of Southern African Studies* 18/1 (March 1992).
Pinnock, Don: *The Brotherhoods: Street Gangs and State Control in Cape Town* (Cape Town: David Philip, 1984).
Ramphele, Mamphela: 'Social disintegration in the black community: implications for social transformation', in Everatt, David and Sisulu, Sheila (eds): *Black Youth in Crisis* (Johannesburg: Ravan, 1992).
Ritchken, Edwin: 'Burning the herbs: Youth politics and witches in Lebowa', *Work in Progress* 48 (July 1987).
Ritchken, Edwin: 'Comrades, witches and the state: the case of the Brooklyn Youth Organisation', paper presented to the African Studies seminar, University of the Witwatersrand, September 1987.
Scharf, Wilfried: 'The Impact of Liquor on the Working-Class (with Particular Focus on the Western Cape)', MSocSci dissertation, University of Cape Town (1984/85).
Scharf, Wilfried and Ngcokoto, Baba: 'Images of punishment in the people's courts of Cape Town', 1985-7', in Manganyi, N Chabani and Du Toit, Andre (eds): *Political Violence and the Struggle in South Africa* (Halfway House: Southern Books, 1990).

Seekings, Jeremy: 'Political Mobilisation in Tumahole, 1984-85', *Africa Perspective*, new series 1/7-8 (October 1989).

Seekings, Jeremy, 'Gender ideology and township politics in the 1980s', *Agenda* 10 (1991).

Sitas, Ari: 'The Making of the Comrades Movement in Natal 1985-91', *Journal of Southern African Studies* 18/3 (September 1992).

Straker, Gill: *Faces in the Revolution: The Psychological Effects of Violence on Township Youth in South Africa* (Cape Town: David Philip, 1992).

Swilling, Mark: '"Because your yard is too big": squatters, the local state, and dual power in Uitenhage, 1985-1986', paper presented at the African Studies Institute seminar, University of the Witwatersrand, March 1988.

The Joint Enrichment Project

The Joint Enrichment Project (JEP) was founded in 1986 by the South African Council of Churches and the Southern African Catholic Bishops' Conference, in response to the alienation of black youth from the disintegrating education system.

In 1991 the JEP became concerned that, despite the success of the back to school campaign in getting large numbers of youth to heed the call to return to school, many others had not returned. They had simply 'dropped out' of education and its institutions.

The tendency to label this group of young people a 'lost generation' and to focus only on the 'politicised' and 'militarised' youth detracted from the huge number of young people who are not necessarily politically active, but are victims of a broad and deep-rooted social disintegration.

The Broederstroom conference

Prompted by these concerns, the JEP convened a conference in June 1991 to place the issue of 'marginalised youth' on the national agenda. The conference was attended by seventy-two organisations representing different sectors and ideologies. The conference expressed concern that so little was known about the marginalised youth: their numbers, needs and aspirations.

The conference mandated the JEP to undertake a broad consultative and research process to ensure that this information was obtained and made available, and to use it to inform the design and planning of appropriate programmes.

Towards a national youth development initiative

☆ *Regional consultation:* since June 1991, the JEP has organised a series of regional consultations. These have elected structures to ensure that programmes which are implemented meet the specific needs of youth in each region.
☆ *National Youth Summit:* a National Youth Summit, attended by eighty youth organisations, was held in June 1992. The recommendations of this summit are being implemented by the National Youth Development Co-ordinating Committee.
☆ *Youth directory:* the JEP has compiled a directory of organisations working with youth in South Africa. The aim of this is to encourage networking, and to ensure that programmes consider the particular needs of marginalised youth.
☆ *Research:* the research which has been undertaken by C A S E, and of which the following study is only the first part, will be used to inform all the above initiatives.

The JEP is adamant that all initiatives address the real, and not the perceived, needs of young people.

The Community Agency for Social Enquiry

The Community Agency for Social Enquiry (C A S E) is an independent research and training resource which has served the progressive movement since 1986.

C A S E has undertaken national policy research for organisations including the South African Council of Churches, the Southern African Catholic Bishops Conference, the Nederduitse Gereformeerde Kerk (Afrika), Cosatu, Sached and a host of other organisations. C A S E also undertakes computer training for progressive organisations, operating from its offices in Johannesburg, Cape Town and Pietermaritzburg.

C A S E provided the research co-ordination for the conference on 'Marginalised Youth' organised by the Joint Enrichment Project (JEP) in June 1991. In September 1991, C A S E was commissioned by the JEP to design and implement a major research project as an integral part of the National Youth Development Programme which flowed from the 'Marginalised Youth' conference.

The C A S E research programme has the following elements:

☆ *Local research database and resource centre*: researchers have been collecting research into youth and youth-related issues from across South Africa. The material is catalogued and data-based in a resource centre which will be housed by the JEP.
☆ *International comparative data:* researchers have visited Botswana, Uganda and Kenya to study youth development as it is taking place on the ground. This includes youth brigades, job-creation schemes, AIDS awareness campaigns, and more. It is planned that further comparative data will be drawn from Central America. Researchers also visited Geneva and London to liaise with the International Labour Organisation, World Health Organisation, United Nations, the Commonwealth Secretariat,

and others.

☆ *National survey:* a national baseline survey is being conducted which will sample youth in all their diversity and allow them to express their own views, their needs, the problems they face, and how effective solutions can be arrived at.

☆ *Publications:* all of the above research will be submitted to the second national conference organised by the JEP, and will be made public. Reports on local research into AIDS, education, the economy and job-creation, violence and social context, as well as an historical overview, will be issued, as will the international comparative reports on Botswana, Kenya and Uganda, and the results of the national survey.